AN ENCYCLOPEDIA OF STRATEGY FOR FORTNITERS

AN UNOFFICIAL GUIDE FOR BATTLE ROYALE

AN ENCYCLOPEDIA OF STRATEGY FOR FORTNITERS

AN UNOFFICIAL GUIDE FOR BATTLE ROYALE

JASON R. RICH

Sky Pony Press
New York

Copyright © 2018 by Hollan Publishing, Inc.

Fortnite® is a registered trademark of Epic Games, Inc.

The Fortnite game is copyright © Epic Games, Inc.

Sky Pony Press books may be purchased in bulk at special discounts for sales promotion, corporate gifts, fund-raising, or educational purposes. Special editions can also be created to specifications. For details, contact the Special Sales Department, Sky Pony Press, 307 West 36th Street, 11th Floor, New York, NY 10018 or info@skyhorsepublishing.com.

Sky Pony® is a registered trademark of Skyhorse Publishing, Inc.®, a Delaware corporation.

Visit our website at www.skyponypress.com.

Authors, books, and more at SkyPonyPressBlog.com.

10 9 8 7 6 5 4 3 2 1

Library of Congress Cataloging-in-Publication Data is available on file.

Cover design by Brian Peterson

Print ISBN: 978-1-5107-4265-9
Ebook ISBN: 978-1-5107-4268-0

Printed in the United States of America

TABLE OF CONTENTS

INTRODUCTION: LET'S GET STARTED

So, you want to become an awesome *Fortnite: Battle Royale* player and win every match you play, and at the same time, defeat every enemy soldier you encounter? Well, good luck! This type of success is going to take a tremendous amount of game-related knowledge, skill, and practice . . . a lot of practice!

The good news is that to gain the knowledge you'll need to dramatically improve your chances of winning matches (whether you're playing *Fortnite: Battle Royale* on a Windows PC, Mac, PlayStation 4, Xbox One, iPhone, iPad, Nintendo Switch, or Android-based mobile device), you're currently holding an information-packed resource in your hands!

Listed in alphabetical order, so you can quickly look up information about *Fortnite: Battle Royale* when you need it, are tons of descriptions, strategies, and pro tips related to exploring, surviving, building, and fighting.

This unofficial guide contains more than 160 detailed entries related to all aspects of *Fortnite: Battle Royale*. It covers how to improve your gaming skills, and how to ultimately win matches and survive. For example, if you need the inside scoop on Anarchy Acres, simply check out the "A" section of **An Encyclopedia of Strategy for Fortniters** and read the section about Anarchy Acres.

For step-by-step guides to mastering *Fortnite: Battle Royale*, be sure to grab copies of **Fortnite Battle Royale Hacks, Fortnite Battle Royale Hacks: Secrets of the Island,** and **Fortnite Battle Royale Hacks: Advanced Strategies** (each sold separately). Each of these full-color strategy guides is written by Jason R. Rich (@JasonRich7), published by Sky Pony Press, and offers hundreds of additional strategies for mastering *Fortnite: Battle Royale*.

Overview of *Fortnite: Battle Royale*

Unless in real life you've been living on your own remote island and have been detached from the world around you, you probably know that *Fortnite: Battle Royale* from Epic Games has become one of the most popular games in the world, and for good reason.

At the start of every match, 100 soldiers are airlifted by the Battle Bus and literally dropped off on a mysterious island with just one primary goal—survival!

Fortnite: Battle Royale combines high-action combat with the need to build, explore, utilize resources, and strategize. Each player controls one soldier throughout each match.

Soldiers are forced to free fall from the Battle Bus.

As land quickly approaches, a glider is activated, allowing for a safe landing. During free fall and once the glider is active, steer your soldier and choose where on the island you want to land.

Using weapons, ammo, loot items, and resources (wood, stone, and metal) that you find and collect on the island, your objective is to be the last person alive at the end of each match. There's no second place. You either survive or you get defeated when experiencing this high-intensity, real-time, massively multiplayer, online-based game.

Each match lasts approximately 15 exciting minutes. During this time, focus on survival and avoid enemy confrontations, or choose to fight every enemy soldier you encounter. If you manage to stay alive until the End Game (the last few minutes of a match), you'll be forced to fight against the small group of remaining soldiers, each of whom wants to survive as badly as you do.

As the safe area of the island gets smaller, all of the surviving soldiers are forced into a more confined area, until the End Game, when the safe area of the island is tiny, and the remaining soldiers must fight each other until there's only one survivor. This map shows the island about halfway through a match. As you can see, a large portion of the island has already been ravaged by the storm. Based on

Oh, and there's a deadly storm to contend with as well. When you first land, the entire island is inhabitable. You can explore anywhere. However, after a few minutes, the deadly storm materializes, and then during each match, it periodically expands and covers more and more of the island—making the land uninhabitable. This is what it looks like when your soldier is caught in the storm. The longer your soldier stays in the storm, the more damage will negatively impact their health and shields.

the location of the inner circle, it appears the safe area will soon be around Pleasant Park.

To survive on the island, you'll need to master a handful of core skills relating to:

- **Building**—Using the resources (wood, stone, and metal) you collect, you're able to build structures, ramps, stairs, shielding barriers, and fortresses that offer protection and can help you stay alive. Knowing what to build, how to design your structures, what resources to use, and when to build are all essential strategies to master.

- **Collecting and Using Weapons, Ammo, Loot, and Resources**—When you land on the island, you're armed only with a pickaxe. You'll need to quickly find and collect weapons, ammo, and loot items to help you successfully fight enemies and protect yourself. You'll also need to collect resources, so you can build.

- **Combat**—Using the weapons, ammo, and loot you collect, it'll be necessary to engage enemy soldiers in battle. Each time you defeat an adversary, you receive Experience Points (XP), as well as all of the weapons, ammo, loot, and resources that the defeated soldier has thus far collected during the match, but has left behind.

- **Exploration**—The island contains more than 20 popular points of interest, along with many areas that are not labeled on the island map. You'll be forced to explore forests, farms, factories, stores, buildings, houses, and many other structures within these points of interest. It's within these structures that you'll often find weapons, ammo, and loot lying on the ground (waiting to be grabbed), as well as chests and ammo boxes. Of course, there's a good chance you'll also encounter enemy soldiers who you'll need to confront and fight, or retreat from quickly.

- **Survival**—Knowing that you need to be the last person remaining alive on the island, it's your job to decide when and where to fight; what weapons, ammo, loot, and resources you'll use; determine where on the island you want to explore; maintain your soldier's health (HP); and avoid the storm—all at the same time.

There are many points of interest to visit on the island, as well as hundreds of different types of weapons to find and collect, and more than a dozen types of loot. *The Ultimate Unofficial Encyclopedia for Fortnite: Battle Royale* explains all the core gaming elements you must become acquainted with, plus offers many tips for surviving and winning matches.

If you want to understand everything right from the start, read this unofficial guide from cover to cover. However, as you're actually playing *Fortnite: Battle Royale*, or if there's something about the game you don't fully understand, simply look it up, and you'll gain vital tactical knowledge that will help you survive.

Remember, during each match, you're battling against up to 99 other players (not computer-controlled opponents.) Based on their individual actions, it'll often be necessary to quickly alter your strategy and react fast to whatever challenges you encounter. This might mean going on the offensive, protecting yourself against an incoming attack, taking cover and hiding, or quickly retreating from the area you're in. Try to keep tabs on the locations of your enemies and anticipate their actions.

Fortnite: Battle Royale Is Continuously Evolving

One of the things that makes *Fortnite: Battle Royale* so exciting, and that keeps the game from becoming repetitive, boring, or easy to master, is the fact that every week or two . . ., Epic Games releases a game update (referred to as a "patch") that introduces new gaming elements, new weapons, new types of loot, additional character customization options, new challenges, and sometimes additional game play modes. Some of these additions become permanent, while others are offered for a limited time and are later discontinued or removed from the game.

In addition, every few months, *Fortnite: Battle Royale* kicks off a new season. With the launch of a new season, new points of interest are added to the map, and more significant updates to the game are introduced.

Fortnite A-Z: The Unofficial Encyclopedia for Fortnite Players was compiled during Season 4. Season 5 began in mid-July 2018. Thus, there will likely be points of interest, weapons, types of loot, and other game play elements that aren't covered within this book, because they didn't yet exist. For the latest news about *Fortnite: Battle Royale*, visit: www.epicgames.com/fortnite/en-US/news.

#1 VICTORY ROYALE

At the end of a match, only one soldier survives. As soon as the surviving soldier defeats the last remaining enemy, #1 Victory Royale appears on the screen and he/she can perform a victory dance and revel in his/her success

Aim Assist

Available from the Settings menu, Aim Assist makes it easier for players using a wireless controller (as opposed to a keyboard/mouse) to aim weapons in *Fortnite: Battle Royale*. This feature can be turned on (making it easier to aim a weapon) or turned off.

Aim Weapon

Anytime you're facing an enemy with a weapon drawn, and you pull the trigger, the bullet travels forward, hopefully hitting your adversary. By pressing the Aim button on the controller (or keyboard/mouse) first, you will zoom in a bit on your target. Here, a rifle with a scope is ready to shoot, but *without* the Aim button pressed.

It's easier to target enemies, and potentially make a more devastating head shot, if you press the Aim button, target your weapon, and then press the trigger to fire. This weapon is aimed at the driver's seat of the truck.

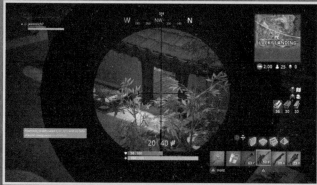

If you're using a rifle with a scope, when you press the Aim button on the controller, this scope view is displayed. It allows you to zoom in on an enemy that's very far away. Use a rifle with a scope for sniping from a distance.

Ambush

When you're within any pre-made building, you always have the option to hide behind furniture or an object, crouch down, aim your weapon, and wait for an enemy to appear. Then, launch a surprise attack to quickly defeat the unsuspecting adversary.

Another way to ambush an opponent is to place remote explosives or a trap somewhere sneaky, where you think an enemy might search. When he or she gets close, manually detonate the remote explosive, or allow the trap to activate by itself. This will damage or potentially defeat an enemy. To lure an enemy into a booby-trapped area, try dropping a few pieces of valuable loot nearby, using it as bait.

Shown here is a remote explosive that has been placed on the wall. It's active. You can tell because its blue light is flashing. The soldier that placed this explosive now needs to get out of the way and wait for an enemy to approach before manually detonating it. See the listing for "Remote Explosives" to get the scoop on this type of weapon.

Ammo

All of the different types of guns you'll find on the island require ammunition. A weapon without ammunition is useless. For your more powerful weapons, conserve ammo until situations when that particular weapon is truly needed. For example, a sniper rifle should be used when you want to pick off enemies from a distance, or a grenade launcher can be used to destroy an enemy's fortress while your adversary is still inside.

Ammo can be collected from ammo boxes, found and picked up from the ground (shown here), acquired from defeated enemies, and collected from chests or Supply Drops. When you see ammo lying on the ground (out in the open), collect it.

At any time, access the Backpack Inventory screen to see the types of ammo you've collected. Keep in mind, there are different types of ammo, and each works with a specific type of gun, rifle, or weapon. From the Backpack Inventory screen, highlight an ammo type to determine which weapon that ammo works with, and how much of it you've collected and have on hand.

Ammo Box

Ammo boxes contain a random assortment of ammo. Unlike a chest, an ammo box does not glow. Look for them mainly in homes, buildings, and other pre-made structures. They're often found on shelves or under staircases, for example.

Anarchy Acres

Found between map coordinates E2.5 and F2.5, Anarchy Acres is one of two farmland areas on the island. Here, you'll come across barns, silos, tractors, stables, and wilted crops.

Explore the large farmhouse to find weapons, ammo, and loot.

Behind haystacks, you might discover hidden items, or an enemy soldier could be crouched down and waiting to attack you. Hiding behind

hay offers no protection whatever if someone shoots at the hay, but it can potentially keep a soldier from being seen.

The buildings and structures in Anarchy Acres are often located a good distance apart. To travel between them, you'll often need to walk or run out in the open. To avoid getting hit by weapons fire, run (don't walk) in a zigzag pattern, and keep jumping up and down. Look for items to hide behind for cover or build a vertical wall or mini-fort to help shield your soldier, if necessary.

As you explore the stables, check out each horse stall for goodies. You can also use one of these areas to crouch down as you wait to ambush an adversary. Build a ramp to reach the loft area and open the chest.

Apples

Scattered randomly throughout the island and found under trees, you'll discover Apples. Walk up to an Apple, and when you see the Consume message appear, eat the Apple to replenish 5HP. You can eat as many Apples in a row as you can find, to replenish your Health meter up to 100 percent.

Typically, you'll find a handful of Apples clustered together under a tree. Grab and consume an Apple if your HP meter is below 100 percent. You must eat an Apple when and where you find it. You can't pick them up and store them in your backpack for later consumption, like you can with other HP powerups, like Bandages or Med Kits.

It takes just a few seconds to consume an Apple, during which time your soldier will be vulnerable to attack, since you can't consume powerups and fire your weapon, move, or build at the same time.

Assault Rifles

There are many types of rifles to find and use against your enemies. The rifle type and rarity will determine how powerful it is. Rifles, especially rifles with a scope, are ideal long-range weapons, although they can be used from any distance.

Rifles typically have a slower reload time, and only hold one or two rounds of ammo in the chamber. If you miss a first shot, you could become vulnerable to an enemy attack as your weapon reloads (assuming you have more ammo). In between shots, your enemy could also move or take cover. See "DPS Rating," "Fire Rate," "Reload Time," and "Weapon Rarity" for more information about how the damage capabilities and power of weapons are rated in *Fortnite: Battle Royale*.

To see the power and capabilities of a particular rifle (or any weapon), access the Backpack Inventory screen. Details about the highlighted weapon (and the ammo you have available for it) are displayed.

Attic

Many houses and mansions located throughout the island have an attic. It's often within the attic you'll discover chests (shown), ammo boxes, and/or other powerful loot. Some attics have multiple hidden rooms, so smash through walls, as needed, to explore everywhere.

There are several ways to reach the attic of a building. For example, land on a roof of a house, building, tower, or structure after jumping from the Battle Bus, and smash your way down using the pickaxe.

Enter a home or mansion from ground level and work your way upwards from inside. (You may need to build a ramp or stairs from the top floor to the attic, and then smash your way through the ceiling using your pickaxe.)

From the outside of a house or mansion, build a ramp from the ground to the roof, climb to the top of the roof, and then use your pickaxe to smash your way down from the roof into the attic.

Auto Material Change

Available from the Settings menu, when turned on, this setting allows you to automatically switch between building materials (wood, stone, or metal) if you run out of the resource you're currently building with, but the

structure you're building isn't yet complete. Turning on this feature could save you valuable seconds while in Building Mode.

Anytime you enter into Building Mode, after selecting which building shape you want to create, select between wood, stone, or metal as your building material. You can keep building as long as you have an ample supply of that material. When you run out, you'll need to switch building materials (either automatically or manually), or go collect additional resources before you can continue building.

Back Bling

From the Locker, one of the customizations you can make to your soldier is the style of their back bling (their backpack). The back bling you choose determines its appearance but has no impact on what it can hold or how it's used within the game.

You're able to customize the appearance of your soldier before every match. From the Lobby, select the Locker. To change the back bling, highlight and select the Back Bling option, found below the Account and Equipment heading.

Once you access the Back Bling menu, all of the different backpack styles you've unlocked, purchased, or collected thus far are displayed. You can purchase new back bling designs from the Item Shop; unlock back

bling by accomplishing daily, weekly, or Battle Pass-related goals or objectives; or by acquiring this type of loot from a free Twitch Prime Pack, for example. (See "Twitch Prime Packs" for more info on these free downloads.)

Backpack

Every soldier carries a backpack. Within it are six slots for carrying a pickaxe, along with five different types of weapons or loot items. A backpack also holds all of the ammo you find and pick up during a match.

From the Backpack Inventory screen, you're able to rearrange the contents of what's inside, so you can make your most useful weapons and items available to you the quickest. Deciding what types of weapons and ammo you'll carry within your backpack at any given time is an important decision. As a match progresses, your needs will definitely change.

The contents of your backpack are displayed in the lower-right corner of the PS4 screen throughout each match. Its position may vary, depending on which gaming platform you're using.

Once the slots in your backpack are filled up, if you want to swap out an item, select and hold what you want to get rid of, and then grab the new item. The item you were holding will be dropped, and the new one will be picked up.

One type of versatile weapon you definitely want to find and keep on hand throughout a match is any type of shotgun. These are more powerful than pistols in close-range combat, but can also be used to shoot at mid-range or distant targets.

Within your backpack, it's also a good idea to hold onto at least one type of HP powerup item that will help to keep your soldier alive if he or she gets injured. Bandages, Cozy Campfires, Chug Jugs, Med Kits, and Slurp Juice are some of the more useful pieces of loot that will help you replenish your Health (HP) meter.

Backpack Inventory

This is the combination of weapons, loot, and ammo that you're carrying around at any given time. In addition to your pickaxe, your backpack has six inventory slots. Each slot can hold one weapon or loot item. It's possible to hold multiples of some loot items, such as Bandages, within a single slot.

At any time, you can drop an item from your backpack in order to pick up something different. For example, once your backpack is filled, you can drop a pistol to pick up a shotgun. Or if you have a few Bandages, you might want to use or drop them, so you can pick up and carry a more powerful Med Kit or Chug Jug that you find.

From the Backpack Inventory screen, you're able to rearrange the contents of your backpack, so your most frequently used weapons and items are easily accessible.

Bandages

Bandages can be found within chests, lying on the ground (often within houses, buildings, or structures), collected from defeated enemies, or found within Supply Drops, for example. Each time you use a Bandage, it replenishes 15 HP (up to 100). Within one backpack slot, you can hold up to 5 Bandages, and then use them individually when they're needed.

It takes several seconds to use Bandages, during which time your soldier will be vulnerable to attack, since he/she can't move, fire a weapon, or build at the same time. Consider crouching behind an object or building walls around your soldier for protection before using Bandages or consuming any health and/or shield-replenishing item.

Basement

Located within many homes, buildings, mansions, and other structures are basements. It's here (and in attics) that you'll often find chests, powerful weapons, as well as useful ammo and loot.

Outside of a home, if you see a cellar door, smash it open with your pickaxe, enter into the basement, and explore. Be sure to look for hidden rooms. From within some homes,

buildings, mansions, and other structures, you'll need to smash through the floor when you're at ground level in order to discover a hidden basement.

Battle Bus

At the start of a match you'll find yourself (along with other soldiers) waiting in the pre-deployment area. Feel free to walk around and explore while waiting to board the Battle Bus, which will transport everyone to the island.

The Battle Bus is a blue bus that flies. It'll take you (and up to 99 other soldiers) from the pre-deployment area directly over the island.

Jump out of the Battle Bus at any time once it's over the island. During freefall, control the direction and speed of your soldier's fall, so you're able to choose a precise landing location.

During free fall, your soldier drops toward land at a steady rate. Use your directional controls to alter their direction. To increase their rate of descent (to reach land faster), point them in a downward direction. The first soldiers to reach land, and then find and grab one or more weapons, will gain a tactical advantage. He/she can shoot unarmed soldiers that land nearby after them.

Battle Bus Route Map

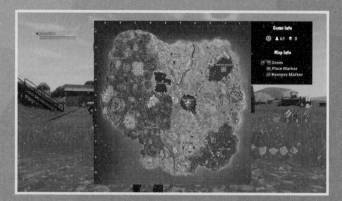

While in the pre-deployment area waiting for the Battle Bus, or once aboard it, press the Map button to access the island map. During this period, a blue line, composed of arrows, is displayed. This line shows the random route that the bus will follow as it travels over the island. Study this map to choose the ideal moment to jump out of the Battle Bus, based on your desired landing location.

Battle Pass

In conjunction with each season, Epic Games offers a Battle Pass for sale. This is a collection of daily, weekly, and tier-based goals and challenges. Each time you complete a goal or challenge, your soldier gains Experience Points (XP) and could unlock loot or character customization items.

Each Battle Pass lasts for one season and contains several Tiers. To acquire a Battle Pass, view its Tiers, and see what items and loot can be unlocked by completing each Tier, from the Lobby, select the Battle Pass option.

To view a list of daily and weekly challenges during each Battle Pass, from the Lobby, access the Challenges screen.

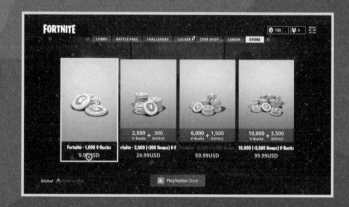

At any time during a season, you can purchase a Battle Pass using V-Bucks (which cost real money). To acquire V-Bucks, visit the Store.

Once you have enough V-Bucks, visit the Battle Pass screen and select the Purchase Battle Pass option. The cost is around $20. However, once you purchase and activate a Battle Pass, if you can't (or don't want to) complete the necessary challenges to unlock the loot and items available, for an additional fee, consider purchasing Battle Pass Tiers. Each Tier you unlock with a purchase (at a cost of 150 V-Bucks) will unlock the loot and limited-edition character customization items that were offered in that Tier.

If you don't want to purchase a Battle Pass, you can continue playing *Fortnite: Battle Royale* for free, but the rewards for completing daily or weekly challenges, or reaching certain Experience Levels, will not be as rare or exciting as what you'd unlock with a purchased Battle Pass.

Battle Pass Tier

Each Tier of a Battle Pass consists of a series of pre-defined daily, weekly, and Tier-related goals or challenges. Access the Battle Pass screen (from the Lobby) to view each Tier and see what will be unlocked by completing it.

Boogie Bombs

This type of weapon can be collected and stored within your backpack. When you opt to use it, toss it directly at an enemy soldier. They'll be forced to dance for five seconds, during which time they'll receive damage.

Builder Pro Controller Layout

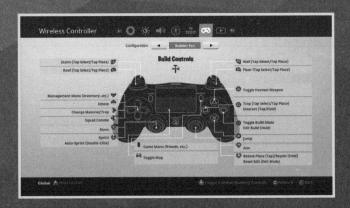

From the Settings menu, select the Wireless Controller option. You're then able to choose between several pre-configured controller layouts. The Builder Pro layout is ideal for a player who has expertise in building and uses this capability as one of their main strategies. This controller layout makes the most popular building tools more readily accessible.

Building Mode

One of the keys to becoming a pro *Fortnite: Battle Royale* player is to be able to quickly switch into and out of Building Mode. While in Building Mode, you must be able to quickly construct forts or structures without thinking too much about it.

The faster you build, the bigger your advantage will be, especially if you're in the midst of a firefight and you're building a ramp or fortress to get higher than your opponent, or for protection (shielding) from an incoming attack.

Once in Building Mode, choose which building piece(s) to create or edit, as well as which resource to build with. Wood is the fastest but offers the least protection. Metal takes longer to build with but offers the most protection. This is what a single vertical wall piece (made of wood) looks like as it's being built.

Building Pieces

After activating Building Mode, choose which resource (wood, stone, or metal) you want to build with, and then choose which building piece you want to create. You can choose between vertical wall pieces, floor/ceiling pieces, ramp/stair pieces, or pyramid-shaped roof pieces. Here, the available building pieces are displayed near the bottom-right corner of the screen, but this will vary, based on which gaming platform you're using.

The key to becoming an expert at building is being able to mix and match building pieces to construct durable and useful structures, ramps, or fortresses, whenever and wherever they're needed. The structure shown here was built using wood, stone, and metal. You can see that each material looks different by

studying this structure. See "Resources" to discover how to collect resources.

The building pieces and structures you can construct are based mainly on how many resources you've collected and your own creativity. Once you get into the End Game phase of a match, you'll discover your adversaries will build tall and often highly creative fortresses—both for protection, and from which they launch their final assaults.

In the End Game or when building a fort or ramp near an opponent, use the same material they're using to build. This will mask the sound of your own building, making it harder for the enemy to pinpoint your exact location.

Using the ramp/stairs piece, quickly build tall ramps/stairs to help you reach otherwise inaccessible areas within a building or structure, for example. You can also create a ramp or stairs to quickly climb up higher than your opponent during a firefight. Typically, the soldier who is higher up has a tactical advantage. Here, a ramp is jutting out of a small wooden fortress.

Once a wall or ceiling piece has been built or you've constructed a fortress, for example, enter into Edit Mode to add a window or door to the structure.

One type of structure you definitely want to learn how to build is a "1x1" fortress.

Learn to Quickly Build "1x1" Fortresses

A 1x1 fortress is simply four walls around you, with a ramp in the center that goes up multiple levels. Using wood allows you to build with the greatest speed, but using metal offers the best protection. Keep practicing until you're able to build this type of fortress very quickly, without having to think too much about it.

Use a door to easily enter/exit a structure. Keep in mind, once you build a door, anyone can pass through it, whether they're invited or not. Use a window to see out of or shoot from. Of course, an enemy can see in through a window and shoot at you as well.

Here's how to build a 1x1 fortress:

Building Techniques

Some *Fortnite* players spend countless hours practicing in Building Mode, to master how to construct elaborate, multi-level fortresses. Others rely more on their fighting and combat skills and utilize Building Mode only when it's absolutely essential.

First build four vertical walls so they surround you.

In the center, build a ramp. As the ramp is being constructed, jump on it. Keep repeating this process to add levels to your fort.

At the top, consider adding four pyramid-shaped roof pieces around the roof for added protection when you peek out. However, if you need protection from directly above as well, be sure to add a roof over your soldier's head.

In many instances, height is more important than security. Build a quick and tall ramp upwards, and then shoot down at enemies below.

Add a vertical wall on both sides of the ramp (near the top) to provide more protection when you're standing at the top and shooting at enemies below you. As long as an enemy does not have time to shoot and destroy your ramp while you're on it, you'll be at an advantage. It's safe for your soldier to fall three stories maximum when leaping out or off of a structure. If he/she falls from any higher, injury (or worse) will result.

When you need quick protection, build a vertical wall with the strongest material you have available, and then quickly build a ramp (or stairs) directly behind it. You can then crouch down directly behind this structure for protection. Doing this provides a double layer of shielding that an enemy will have to shoot through and destroy in order to reach you. By crouching down, you become a smaller target.

In some cases, building two ramps, side-by-side, gives you an advantage. First, an opponent can't see your exact location when you move back and forth between ramps. Also, if one ramp is about to get destroyed, quickly leap to the other to survive the attack and avoid falling. Yes, this requires more resources, but it's often worth it.

A "ramp rush" is a strategy that involves building a tall ramp quickly, so you're able to move directly toward and over an enemy (or their fort) to initiate an attack. Using the double-wide ramp and zigzagging between them makes it harder for your enemies to track your exact location.

Buildings & Structures Found on the Island

Throughout the island, you'll find many houses and mansions to explore and potentially hide or fight within. On the outside, the homes and mansions may all look different. However, on the inside, all offer several levels, and on each level, you'll discover several rooms and hallways to explore. Some homes, for example, also have an attic and/or basement.

In addition to homes and mansions, various points of interest on the island also offer tall buildings, farm houses, factories, mines, prisons, indoor sports arenas, stores, restaurants, gas stations (shown), towers, churches, and other types of pre-created structures.

Anytime you're about to enter a building, listen carefully for movement coming from the inside. You might hear an enemy's footsteps, doors opening/closing, or an adversary using their pickaxe to smash things. Whatever the case, if you hear movement and still choose to enter that structure, do so with your weapon drawn. Also consider tiptoeing, so you generate less noise.

Before entering a building, peek through the window, if possible. If you see an enemy, shoot through the window or toss a grenade.

Almost any building or structure you discover on the island can be smashed using a pickaxe and used to collect resources. This includes the walls, floors, and ceilings, as well as any contents inside (such as furniture or machinery). If you know an enemy is hiding within a building and you have a projectile explosive weapon at your disposal (or some type of grenade or remote explosive), use that weaponry to blow up the building and whomever is inside. Here, instead of walking through the front door, the front wall of the house was smashed apart and demolished.

When you approach a house, building, or structure and see the door is already open, this means someone is currently inside, or has already searched that structure and has left. If they're still inside, consider waiting outside, so you can launch a surprise attack, defeat the enemy as they leave, and collect all of their weapons, ammo, loot, and resources. If you choose to enter the structure, do so with extreme caution and with your weapon drawn. You'll likely encounter one or more enemies inside and be forced into a firefight within a confined space.

Regardless of the building or structure you're in, use Building Mode to build inside. For example, build a vertical wall inside a building for protection, or build a ramp (or stairs) to help you reach an otherwise inaccessible area.

Bush

Use a bush as a hiding spot. Walk up to it and crouch down inside. Depending on the size of the bush, you can go unseen by nearby enemies. However, if you do get spotted, the bush offers zero protection from incoming weapon fire.

Once a soldier has activated the bush loot item and is hiding within the bush (staying still), he can't be seen by onlookers. However, if one of your enemies notices a moving bush, he's very likely to attack, so use this item with caution when you want to avoid detection. Remain still.

It's also possible to find and collect a bush as loot. This is an item you can carry with you in your backpack. When you use it, your soldier will wear the bush as camouflage in order to blend in with their outdoor surroundings. Crouch down so you remain unseen. When using the bush loot item, you can move around freely while wearing it.

With the bush loot item active, crouch down. You're able to target and shoot a weapon from within the bush. Remember, if someone shoots back, the bush offers zero protection.

Bush Camping

Bush camping is a strategy where you simply hide in a bush (in the safe area of the circle), waiting for the other enemy soldiers to battle and defeat each other, while your soldier remains safely hidden until the End Game portion of a match. When you hide within a bush, or use the bush camouflage item, you are almost entirely hidden, even when an enemy comes close to your location.

Campground

This is one of the areas that are not labeled on the map. You'll find it near map coordinates I5.5. Here you'll find RVs and dumpsters, which are a great source for metal. There are also a handful of small structures to explore and plenty of items to find and collect, including chests and powerful weapons.

Cars and Trucks

Throughout the island, you'll see many abandoned cars, trucks, tractors, ice cream trucks, buses, RVs, and other vehicles. These can serve several purposes.

Crouch behind vehicles for protection when someone is shooting at you, or when you're shooting at someone else.

Using your pickaxe, smash vehicles (including cars, buses, vans, and trucks) to collect metal. These are one of the best sources of metal on the island. The drawback, however, is that when you start smashing a vehicle, it makes a lot of noise, and will help a nearby enemy determine your location. Often, when you start smashing a car, you'll hear its alarm go off, which makes even more noise.

You'll sometimes find chests hidden in the backs of trucks and other types of vehicles. Don't forget to search on top of trucks. You'll sometimes find additional weapons, ammo, or loot.

Character Customization

There are several customizations you can make to the appearance of your soldier. From the Locker, start by choosing his or her outfit.

C

This is the clothing worn during a match. You're also able to select separate back bling, which determine the appearance of their backpack.

Next, choose the design of your glider (and related contrail animation), the appearance of your pickaxe, and what emotes (including dance moves) your soldier can publicly showcase during a match.

Remember, the customizations you make to your solider only impact how he/she looks in the game. While you can spend real money to make your soldier appear truly awesome and very unique, this is optional.

Most gamers love the ability to customize the appearance of their soldier. For example, you can select their outfit, back bling, glider design, pickaxe design, contrail animation, and up to six different emotes. Customizing your soldier's appearance can be done before each match. From the Lobby, access the Locker, and then choose the Outfit option (shown here). Only outfits you've unlocked, previously acquired, or have purchased will be available.

The options available to you in the Locker are based on what you've unlocked during gameplay, what you've purchased from the Item Shop, and what you've downloaded (for free) from Twitch Prime Packs, for example. Items from the Item Shop are purchased one at a time using V-Bucks.

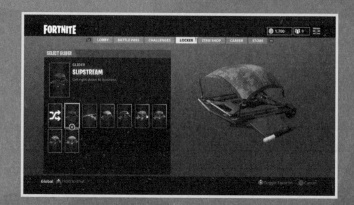

If you select the glider option from the Locker, a selection of the glider designs you've unlocked, purchased, or acquired are displayed. Choose one from the menu and confirm your choice.

Every day, a different selection of customizable options (including outfits, glider designers, pickaxe designs, and emotes) are available for sale from the Item Shop. Purchase one item at a time using V-Bucks. These items ultimately cost real money and are typically only available for a very limited time.

Plan on spending between $5.00 and $25.00 for a single outfit, or more if you want to add matching back bling and a pickaxe design.

The rare and slick-looking Venturion outfit, for example, costs 1,500 V-Bucks. The matching Triumph Glider design costs an extra 500 V-Bucks, while the matching Airfoil pickaxe design will set you back another 800 V-Bucks.

Click on the Store menu option to purchase V-Bucks that you can exchange for items or Battle Passes. Purchasing 1,000 V-Bucks costs $9.99. Thus, this particular outfit, priced at 1500 V-Bucks, actually costs approximately $15 (US). It would be cheaper, however, if you use V-Bucks you've won within the game and/or purchased in bundles of more than 1,000. See the "V-Bucks" listing for more information.

Chests

All chests contain a random selection of weapons, ammo, loot, and/or bundles of resources. You'll typically find chests hidden within houses and buildings throughout the island, but occasionally, they're found out in the open as well.

Once you locate a chest, walk up and open it. Depending on its location, you may need to crouch down to open a chest. The chest's contents will scatter out on the ground. Based on what you already have within your backpack, pick and choose the weapons, ammo, loot, and resource items you want to grab, and if necessary, replace unwanted items in your backpack with new ones.

When you're exploring a building, listen carefully for the special sound a chest makes as you get close to it, and always be on the lookout for their golden glow.

Sometimes, to reach a chest that's hidden within a building or structure, you'll need to build a ramp or stairs to reach it. If a chest is hidden in an attic, it may be necessary to get to the outside roof and then use your pickaxe to smash downward (through the roof) into the attic.

If you're inside a building and can't figure out how to reach the attic, go to the top floor and build a ramp to the ceiling. Use your pickaxe to smash upwards through the ceiling.

Throughout the island, the location of chests is usually the same from match to match. So, once you find a chest, remember its location. During a future match, return to that location and open the chest to collect what's inside. In some of the island's points of interest, the location of the chests is somewhat random. Once a chest is opened during a match, it rarely respawns. The first soldier to reach and open a chest is the one who receives its contents.

Sometimes, you'll discover chests sitting out in the open, or they could be hidden inside or behind something. Here, a chest is hidden outside within this dog house.

If you choose to approach a chest that's out in the open, do so with extreme caution. There could be an enemy soldier armed with a sniper rifle hidden nearby waiting for you to approach the chest. As soon as you're seen, you'll get shot. Be prepared to quickly build barrier walls around yourself for protection as you open a chest that's located in a spot that makes you vulnerable to attack.

Chug Jug

When you consume a Chug Jug, your Health *and* Shield meters get replenished to 100 percent. A Chug Jug takes 15 seconds to consume.

During this time, your soldier can't move around, build, or fire a weapon. They're vulnerable to attack. Before consuming a Chug Jug, find a secluded or secure location.

Drink a Chug Jug early in a match to fully charge your Health and Shields meters, and then save at least one until the End Game portion of a match, when survival becomes more difficult and having 100% health and shields will keep you alive longer.

Circle

The area within the outer circle of the island map is currently the safe (inhabitable) area of the island. This area has not yet been ravaged by the storm. The area in pink is the uninhabitable area, where the storm is already active.

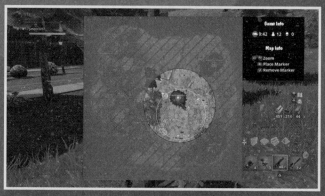

When you see two circles on a map, the area within the outer circle is currently the safe area. The area within the inner circle shows you the impact the storm will have the next time it expands and moves. A white line indicates the most direct route to follow so that you stay out of the storm.

Clingers

These explosive weapons look like a toilet plunger and can be collected and stored in your soldier's backpack. When you want to use one, select it as the active weapon, and then toss it directly at your enemy or any nearby object.

Once a Clinger is thrown, it will stick directly to an enemy soldier or nearby object (such as a wall or tree). It will turn blue, indicating it's been activated. Then, within a few seconds, it'll explode! Anyone caught in the explosion will be injured (or worse).

Clingers will stick to almost anything, and once they've attached to a soldier or object, they can't be removed. To increase the damage these explosive weapons cause, quickly throw two or more of them at the same target, and then take cover!

Combat Pro Controller Layout

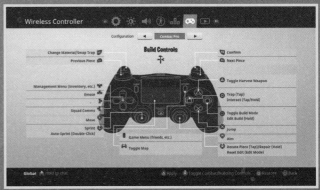

If your primary strategy when playing *Fortnite: Battle Royale* is combat, and you're playing on a PS4 or Xbox One, consider switching your wireless controller layout to Combat Pro. This makes the most commonly used fighting features more readily available to you. From the Lobby, access the Settings menu, and then choose the Wireless Controller submenu.

Contrail

This is the animation you see trailing behind your soldier as he/she free falls from the Battle Bus toward the island. You're able to unlock a wide range of contrail designs and patterns.

Cozy Campfire

Cozy Campfires are rare, but when you find one, save it for when you, or you and your allies (if you're playing Duos or Squad Mode), need healing. Collect a Cozy Campfire from Chests, Supply Drops, or defeated enemies, and then store it in your backpack until it's needed.

To activate a Cozy Campfire, you must be on a flat surface, so consider entering into Building Mode and creating one floor tile, especially if you're outdoors. Select and activate the Cozy Campfire, and then stand directly next to the flame. For each second you're close to the flame (for up to 25 seconds), your HP increases by 2.

Since it'll take you at least 30 seconds to set up and reap the full benefits of a Cozy Campfire, and you're vulnerable to attack while you're using it, build four walls around yourself for added protection, or make sure you're in a secluded and secure area. Any of your allies that also stand next to the flame will have their HP increased as well.

Crossbows

This is a relatively rare short-to-mid-range weapon. Instead of shooting bullets, it uses arrows. As of June 2018, these weapons have been removed from the game, but could make a return at anytime.

Crouch

At any time, your soldier has the ability to crouch down. Do this to hide behind an object to make yourself a smaller target. When you crouch down and move around, this allows you to tiptoe. You'll move slower but make a lot less noise.

As you're exploring indoor areas where enemies may be lurking, tiptoeing around makes it much harder for someone to hear you approaching, and makes you a smaller target if you're spotted.

There will be times when you need to crouch down in order to pass under an object or open a chest (or ammo box), based on where it's positioned.

Regardless of what type of weapon you're using, when you crouch down before aiming and firing that weapon, your accuracy improves.

Customization HUD (*Fortnite Mobile*)

If you're playing *Fortnite: Battle Royale* on an iPhone, iPad, or Android-based smartphone or tablet, you have the ability to fully customize the touchscreen controls.

To access the Customization HUD menu, from the Lobby screen, tap on the menu icon that's located in the top-right corner of the screen. It looks like three horizontal lines.

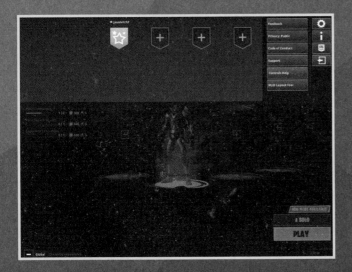

From the menu, tap on the HUD Layout Tool option.

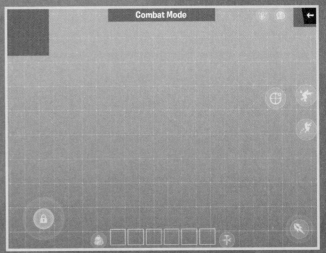

Using your finger, drag the various control icons around on the screen and place each of them, one at a time, in the desired location. This is the default layout for Combat Mode.

Based on how you hold your mobile device, and whether you're right- or left-handed, choose the ideal location for each icon. This is a matter of personal preference. Choose a location for each icon that's easy for you to reach, and that's intuitive, without having to look around on the screen when you're engaged in a match.

Press the left-pointing arrow icon in the top-right corner of the screen to access commands for adjusting the size of each icon. When you're done, again tap on the left-pointing arrow icon that's displayed in the top-right corner of the screen. To save your changes, tap on the Save and Exit button. Your new screen layout will remain active until you manually change or reset it.

Customized Controls

If you're playing *Fortnite: Battle Royale* on a console-based gaming system, such as the PS4, Xbox One, or Nintendo Switch, to customize the wireless controller layout, access the Controller menu.

To do this, from the Lobby, access the Settings menu. On the PS4, for example, press the Options button to access the main menu, and then highlight and select the gear-shaped Settings menu.

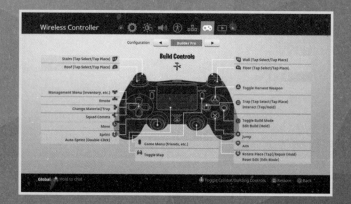

From the Settings menu, scroll to the Controller submenu. Choose a wireless controller layout. Options include Old School (formally known as Standard), Quick Builder, Combat Pro, or Builder Pro. Choose the layout that best fits your personal gaming style, and that makes the features you use the most easily accessible.

If you're playing *Fortnite: Battle Royale* on a Windows PC or Mac and using a keyboard and mouse instead of a controller, from the Settings menu, choose the Keyboard/Mouse option. You can then associate specific keyboard keys or mouse controls with specific commands and movements available within the game. For most players, however, the default settings work very well, so there's no need to tinker with these settings.

Once you make changes to the controller or keyboard/mouse layout, be sure to save your changes. To reset the active layout to their default settings, choose the Restore option that's displayed near the bottom of the Wireless Controller menu screen.

Whatever controller or keyboard/mouse layout you select, memorize that layout so you can quickly access important features, move your soldier around, or switch between fighting and building mode, for example. If you waste valuable seconds trying to figure out which button to press in order to achieve something, you'll wind up getting defeated by an opponent in no time.

Daily Items

Every day, Epic Games offers a new selection of outfits and related character customization items (such as limited edition back bling or pickaxe designs). These are made available for sale from the Item Shop. The items sold within the Item Shop are typically only available for a short time.

Access the Item Shop from the Lobby. On the left side of the screen, you'll see one or two featured outfits (each sold separately). A graphic showing what an outfit looks like, its name, as well as its price (in V-Bucks) is displayed within a rectangular box. If you want to purchase it, highlight and select the box.

You'll be asked to confirm your purchase decision, assuming you have enough V-Bucks to make the purchase. (You can purchase additional V-Bucks, using real money, from the Shop.) Here, the Dragon Axe pickaxe design is about to be purchased for 800 V-Bucks.

In conjunction with each new outfit, a matching glider and pickaxe design is typically offered and sold separately. This is displayed to the immediate right, in a rectangular box next to the daily outfit. The daily outfit and related glider and pickaxe design are considered Featured Items. To the right, you'll notice a section of six additional items, labeled Daily Items, each of which can be purchased separately.

The Daily Items might include additional (optional) outfits, as well as pickaxe or glider designs. Often, at least one or two new emotes are also offered for sale. Again, all of the customization options for your character are for appearance purposes only. None actually give your soldier a competitive advantage during a match. However, altering your soldier's appearance can make him or her look truly unique.

Once an outfit, back bling design, glider design, or emote is purchased and unlocked, it becomes available within your Locker. Access the Locker from the Lobby in order to customize the appearance of your soldier before a match, using outfits and items that you've previously purchased, acquired, or unlocked.

Damage Rating

This is a numeric rating, based on how much potential damage a weapon can cause per direct hit. Always choose an appropriate type of weapon for the task at hand, and one with the highest Damage Rating available to you.

Every weapon offered in *Fortnite: Battle Royale* is categorized by type, and then rated in a variety of ways so gamers can more easily determine the impact it'll have on opponents when used.

These ratings, however, don't take into account a player's aiming accuracy, or differentiate between a body shot versus a headshot. A successful headshot always causes more damage than a body shot.

Once you've selected a weapon to carry, access the Backpack Inventory screen to see detailed information about that particular weapon and how much ammunition you have available for it. Only do this when your soldier is secure and not vulnerable to an enemy attack.

There are plenty of websites, including IGN.com (www.ign.com/wikis/fortnite/Weapons), Gameskinny.com (www.gameskinny.com/9mt22 /complete-fortnite-battle-Royale-weapons-stats-list), and RankedBoost.com (https:// rankedboost.com/fortnite/best-weapons-tier-list), that provide the current stats for each weapon offered in *Fortnite*, based on the latest tweaks made to the game. Just make sure when you look at this information online, it refers to the most recently released version of *Fortnite: Battle Royale*.

Dance Moves

This is one of three types of emotes that allow your soldier to express himself (or herself) while in the pre-deployment area or anytime during a match. Many different dance moves can be unlocked and used. Create your own elaborate choreography by mixing and matching dance move emotes. Use them to distract enemies, brag after a win, or entertain onlookers.

Defeat Opponent

Each time you engage an enemy soldier in battle and win, he or she will be defeated and eliminated from the match. At that time, all of the weapons, ammo, loot, and resources that the soldier was carrying drops to the ground and becomes available for you (or anyone else in the area) to take.

Upgrading your arsenal with weapons, ammo, and loot from defeated enemies potentially gives you access to more powerful items than what you previously had at your disposal. Plus, when you collect a defeated enemy's resources, this saves you a lot of time, since you won't have to harvest as much wood, stone, and metal yourself.

Defeating enemies is one of the fastest ways to increase your character's Experience Level, since this will earn you Experience Points (XP).

DPS Rating

DPS stands for "Damage Per Second." Use this rating to help estimate a weapon's power and damage capabilities. It does not take into account things like accuracy of your aim, or the extra damage you can inflict by making a headshot, for example. In general, DPS is calculated by multiplying the damage the weapon can cause (its Damage Rating) by its Fire Rate.

The rarity of a weapon contributes heavily to its Damage Per Second (DPS) rating. Thus, the DPS rating for a "legionary" weapon is much higher than the DPS rating for an identical weapon that has a "common" rarity. See "Weapon Rarity" for more information.

Duos Mode

Like Solo and Squads, this is one of *Fortnite: Battle Royale*'s game play modes that's always available.

From the Lobby, highlight and select the Game Play Mode option displayed above the Play option, and then choose which Game Play Mode you want to experience.

Select Duos Mode to team up with one friend and confront up to 98 other opponents. The friend you select must be an active *Fortnite* player who is currently online and connected to the game. If you plan to invite a friend, select the "Don't Fill" option after selecting Duos Mode.

After selecting Duos Mode, you can choose your partner, or have the game assign you a partner by selecting the "Fill" option. Once you and your partner are working together, communication throughout the match is essential. Ideally, you both want to be using a gamer's headset, so you can communicate with each other using your voices.

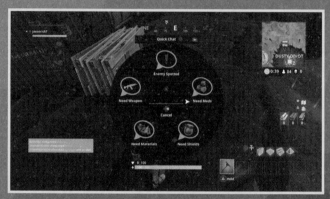

Another way to communicate with other gamers during a match is using the Quick Chat menu. Access it anytime while in the pre-deployment area or on the island during a match. From here, you can send the equivalent to an instant message to your team members. Messages include: "Enemy Spotted," "Need Weapon," "Need Materials," "Need Shields," and "Need Meds."

Dusty Divot

During Season 4 (which kicked off in May 2018), the island was pummeled by what appeared to be comets from outer space. Craters began appearing throughout the island. The largest comet destroyed the area formally known as Dusty Dunes, and in its place, Dusty Divot was built. This area can be found at map coordinates G5.

There are two large buildings (warehouses) on the outskirts of the crater. While you'll be able to stock up on weapons, ammo, and loot, plus find a few chests, you'll often have to fight enemy soldiers in order to stay alive.

Within the crater itself are Hop Rocks (at least during Season 4). When a soldier consumes one of these, for about 30 seconds, he'll be able to jump higher and leap farther. This ability can be used to your tactical advantage, to quickly approach enemies and launch an ambush. However, if Hop Rocks are consumed by your enemies, it'll give them superpowers as well, which can be used against you.

In the center of the massive crater is a research facility. Once you enter, you'll need to navigate through maze-like tunnels to reach the various offices and labs.

Behind each closed door, you may find a lab that's filled with useful items to collect, or you could discover an enemy soldier waiting to pummel you with their weapons, so be prepared for whatever you encounter, and keep your weapon drawn.

Located in the center of the research lab is the comet, which is clearly being studied, or perhaps its power is somehow being harnessed. The secrets this comet holds will likely be revealed during Season 5 (or beyond). What will happen to Dusty Divot in the future is anyone's guess.

Because Dusty Divot in centrally located on the map and is one of the most popular points of interest in the game, if you choose to land here, you must be able to find and grab a weapon within seconds, or you'll be defeated almost instantly.

If Dusty Divot is your desired landing location, one option is to land in a less populated area, somewhere in the outskirts of this point of interest. Collect weapons, ammo, and loot, and then when you're fully armed and prepared to fight, approach Dusty Divot. Consume a Hop Rock found in the outer perimeter of the comet, and then take giant leaps in order to approach the research facility quickly. By doing this, you'll spend less time out in the open and vulnerable to attack.

Emote

While you're in the pre-deployment area, or anytime during a match while you're on the island, you can communicate with your adversaries using three types of emotes.

Emotes must first be unlocked within the game, and then added to your customized Emotes menu from the Locker prior to any match. The Emotes menu has six slots. After unlocking various types of emotes, choose which one goes into each slot. Emotes can be unlocked by purchasing them, by completing challenges or Battle Pass Tiers, or by acquiring them through promotions.

Access the Locker screen, highlight and then select one of the emotes boxes. From the Emotes menu, choose which previously unlocked emote you want to add to that slot.

Graphic emotes allow you to toss a graphic icon into the air for all to see.

An animated dance move allows you to start dancing. Many gamers use this to taunt an enemy or to brag after a victory. There are many different dance moves to unlock and then use, and more are always being introduced.

Once unlocked, a spray paint tag emote allows you to leave your mark on any flat surface on the island using virtual spray paint. Choose a design, and then add it to walls or other objects. Two different designs (an arrow and hearts) were used on this roof.

End Game

The End Game refers to the portion of a match that takes place during the final minutes, when the circle has become extremely small, and only a few highly skilled soldiers remain alive.

It's during the End Game that most gamers opt to build a tall and study fortress, which they'll use for protection and from which they'll launch their attacks using projectile weapons and long-range weapons. Here, a rocket launcher is being used to destroy the opponent's fort.

There are several approaches you can take to defeat an enemy hiding within a fort. You can use a sniper rifle or long-range weapon to target them when they peek out of their fort. Another option is to use a projectile explosive weapon, such as a grenade launcher, to blow up and destroy the fort from a distance (and hopefully take out the enemy as well). Yet another option is to focus on destroying the lower level of a fort, so that the whole thing crashes to the ground, causing your enemy to experience a fatal fall.

Some more gutsy gamers opt to rush enemy forts, using grenades, remote explosives, or whatever weapons are at their disposal as they launch a close-range attack.

Step one is to be prepared. Go into the final circle with your Health and Shield meters fully charged. Plus, have plenty of resources on hand (at least 1,000 to 1,500 wood, stone, and/or metal is ideal). It's also necessary to have the right assortment of weapons in your arsenal. A grenade launcher and/or rocket launcher, as well as a sniper rifle (or rifle with a scope), are definitely must-have weapons.

Notice the location of this particular gamer as the End Game quickly approached. As you can see from the map in the corner of the screen, he was outside the final circle, but invested a lot of resources to build an elaborate fort. According to the timer, he needed to evacuate in about one minute in order to safely reach the final circle and avoid the storm. Thus, he wasted a bunch of resources to build such an elaborate fort at this location.

This is what the island map looks like during the final minutes of an End Game. Notice that almost the entire island, except for a tiny area (between map coordinates H4 and I4) has been consumed by the storm. The three remaining soldiers have been pushed into a very small area and forced into battle.

12 End Game Strategies to Help You Prepare to Win Any Match

Preparation is key when you enter into the End Game in hopes of winning a match. It's important to stay calm, watch what your enemies are doing, and stay focused on your objectives.

Here are 12 End Game strategies to help you win:

1. Choose the best location to build your fortress, from which you'll make your final stand in battle. If you're in a good position, you can be more aggressive with your attacks. However, if you're in the dead center of the final circle, you will become the center of attention, which probably isn't good.
2. Make sure your fortress is tall, well-fortified, and that it offers an excellent, 360-degree view of the surrounding area from the top level.
3. If your fortress gets destroyed, be prepared to move quickly, and have a backup strategy in place that will help to ensure your survival. Having the element of surprise for your attacks gives you a tactical advantage. Don't become an easy target to hit. Keep moving around your fort, or while you're out in the open!
4. During the End Game, don't engage every remaining player. Allow them to fight amongst themselves to reduce their numbers, plus reduce or even deplete their ammo and resources.
5. Only rely on a sniper rifle (or scoped rifle) to make long-range shots if you have really good aim. Otherwise use explosive weapons that'll cause damage over a wide area, such as a grenade launcher or rocket launcher.
6. Always keep tabs on the location of your remaining enemies during the End Game. Don't allow them to sneak up behind you, for example. Even if your back is to the storm, an enemy could enter the storm temporarily, and then emerge behind you to launch a surprise attack if you lose track of their location. Gamers that use the storm to their tactical advantage are referred to as "storm riders" or "storm troopers." If you lose track of an enemy who you know is nearby, listen carefully for their movement.

7. Don't invest a lot of resources into a massive and highly fortified fortress until you know you're in the final circle during a match. Refer to the map and the displayed timer. Otherwise, when the storm expands and moves, you could find it necessary to abandon your fort and then build another one quickly, in a not-so-ideal location. Having to rebuild could use up your resources.

8. Base pushers are enemies that aren't afraid to leave their fortress and attempt to attack yours during the final minutes of a match. Be prepared to deal with their close-range threat.

9. If two or three enemies remain, focus on one at a time. Determine who appears to be the most imminent and largest threat. Be prepared to change priorities at a moment's notice, based on the actions of your enemies.

10. Some final battles take place on ramps, not from within fortresses. In this situation, speed/quick reflexes, getting higher up than your enemy, and good aim with the proper weapon are the keys to winning.

11. Have a Chug Jug on hand to replenish your health and shields if you're attacked and incur damage but are not defeated. Make sure you're well protected when you drink the Chug Jug. Med Kits are also great for maintaining HP during End Games.

12. Study the live streams created by expert *Fortnite* players (on YouTube and Twitch.tv) to learn their End Game strategies and see how they react to various challenges.

Experience Points (XP)

There are many ways to earn XP during a match, including just participating in matches (and not leaving a match early). The longer you stay alive, the more XP you receive. You also receive XP for successful enemy attacks (i.e., causing damage to an enemy), and for each enemy soldier you actually defeat.

XP (or an XP Modifier) can also be earned by completing certain daily, weekly, or Battle Pass-related objectives. By unlocking an XP Modifier, you will receive bonus XP during each match for the remainder of the Battle Pass Tier (or the entire Battle Pass).

Earning XP helps you to increase your Experience Level, which is displayed in the Lobby. One way to see the impact an XP Modifier is having on your success is to access the Profile screen. To reach it from the Lobby, select the Career option, and then highlight and select the Profile option.

Exploration

During any match, one of your primary objectives is exploration of the island. Depending on your strategy, this might mean visiting one or more points of interest and then exploring each of the homes, buildings, and/or structures in that area.

Exploration could also mean searching the less popular areas of the island, in the outskirts of the various points of interest. Collect weapons, ammo, loot, and resources you discover lying on the ground, out in the open, or within the random buildings and structures you encounter. This particular house is located outside of Greasy Grove.

Like everything else on the island, exploration can be dangerous. Avoid accidentally falling off a cliff or tower, for example. Any fall that's higher than three stories could be fatal. Falls from lesser heights, however, often cause HP damage. Shields do not protect a soldier from falls.

Instead of jumping off a tall and steep cliff, you can safely slide down.

Especially if there are enemy soldiers in the same vicinity as you on the island, it's always a good idea to stay on the higher ground. If you're on the roof of a building, and you want to reach the roof of a neighboring building, instead of going down to ground level, entering the other building, and then climbing back up in the second building, consider building a bridge between the roofs of the two buildings.

The quickest way to travel across water, such as the lake area of Loot Lake, is to build a bridge and walk across it. Walking through water is a slow process, and it leaves you out in the open and vulnerable to attack.

Anytime you're exploring inside of a home, building, or structure, your soldier will make noise. If you know enemies are in the immediate area, tiptoe around, and avoid smashing objects with your pickaxe.

Also, whenever you open or close a door, this too makes a sound that can be heard by others who are nearby. To confuse or mislead your enemies, consider closing doors behind you after you open and pass through them.

One of the best ways to get a bird's eye view of an area is to quickly build a tall ramp, climb to the top, and look around. If there are enemies in the area, they'll definitely see the ramp, so be prepared to take cover or shoot at them.

When you see an enemy at the top of a tall ramp, one strategy is to attempt to destroy the bottom of that ramp, so the whole thing comes crashing down. (Remember, a fall from a great height will cause a soldier to perish.)

Fatal Fields

Found at map coordinates G8.5, as you explore this region, you'll discover it's a second, rather large farming area. The farmhouse, silos, barn, and stable, as well as the farm's other structures, are far apart from each other. To reach each of them, you'll need to spend time out in the open and will be vulnerable to attack. Be prepared to hide behind objects, or build walls to use as shields, in case you're attacked.

smashing or shooting at the hay, you'll sometimes discover useful goodies. However, there could just as easily be an enemy soldier waiting to launch an attack from behind a haystack. It's also possible to stand on hay bundles, so you can be a bit higher than ground level (to give yourself a tactical and visual advantage).

Search the large farmhouse carefully. Inside the bathroom, smash your way into a hidden room that contains a chest.

When Fatal Fields is one of the first or last places the Battle Bus passes over, this point of interest tends to become even more crowded than usual, which means you're more apt to encounter enemy soldiers and be forced to fight.

Anytime you're out in the open and need to travel a great distance, run fast, in a zigzag and unpredictable formation, and keep jumping in order to make yourself a difficult target to hit.

Inside the large barn, you'll discover piles of hay. While you can crouch down and hide behind hay, this offers no protective shielding. By

There are two silos on this farm. Land on the top of one and then smash your way down. Inside you'll likely find a chest, or potentially other useful weapons, ammo, or loot.

You're also able to stand at the bottom of a silo and smash it with your pickaxe to reveal what's hidden inside.

Fighting Mode

Fighting mode means you're holding a weapon (any type of gun), or an item (such as a grenade, trap, or remote explosives) that can be used as a weapon, and you're prepared to aim and fire.

Once two or more weapons are stored within slots of your backpack, you can easily switch between them. It's only possible to have one active weapon (in your hands) at a time. Thus, organizing your backpack, so you can quickly grab whichever weapon you need, is essential.

While you'll have the best aim if you crouch down before targeting and firing your weapon, you can use a weapon while you're standing up, walking, running, crouching, jumping, or tiptoeing. However, the faster you're moving, the poorer your aim will be.

During those first few seconds when you land on the island and you're unarmed, or anytime you run out of ammo and find yourself in close proximity to an enemy, you have two choices. First, you can go on the offensive and use your pickaxe as a short-range weapon. Each successful hit will do a small amount of damage to your opponent, so you'll need to whack 'em multiple times for the attack to be fatal. Your second option is simply to run and try to avoid being shot at as you leave the area.

Fire Rate

When it comes to determining how powerful a weapon is, its Fire Rate refers to the number of bullets (or ammo rounds) the weapon can fire per second. Some of the most powerful weapons have a slow Fire Rate, so to inflict the most damage, your aim needs to be perfect. Otherwise, during the time it takes in between shots, your enemy could move, or launch their own counter attack.

If a weapon, like some type of machine gun, has a fast fire rate, you can hold down the trigger and make it rain bullets on your enemy. How effective this is will depend on several factors, including the accuracy of your aim, the rarity of the weapon, the amount of ammo you have on hand for that weapon, and your distance from the opponent.

Flush Factory

Found at map coordinates D9.5, this is an abandoned, multi-level toilet factory. Inside, explore the manufacturing area, as well as the offices and restrooms. There's plenty of useful loot to find and gather inside.

Inside the factory, build stairs or a ramp to reach the top of these restrooms, where you'll likely discover a chest.

The factory itself is several levels tall, with a lot of open area in the middle. If there are enemies lurking around, try to stay in the higher areas, so you can shoot at or defend against enemies below you.

Located near Flush Factory (near map coordinates E9) are a group of buildings that aren't labeled on the map.

The building with the red ropes outside is a dance club. You can spend time dancing on the dance floor, but you'll be more productive if you search the area for loot.

There's often a chest located behind the DJ booth that's located at the end of the dance floor. Each of the other buildings in this area also offers useful weapons, ammo, loot, and occasionally chests. Be sure to check the trucks and metal containers found on the streets in this area.

Fortnite: Battle Royale

This is a free, real-time, massively multiplayer game that takes place on an island. If you purchase the *Fortnite* game, it comes with a series of *Fortnite: Save the World* missions, which are story-based, and vastly different. *Fortnite: Save the World* is separate from *Fortnite: Battle Royale*. By 2019, Epic Games is expected to make *Fortnite: Save the World* a free game as well on all popular gaming platforms.

If you haven't already done so, you can download *Fortnite: Battle Royale* onto your PC or Mac by visiting www.fortnite.com and clicking on the "Get Fortnite" button. PlayStation 4 users should visit the PlayStation Store, while Xbox One users should visit the Xbox Marketplace. Visit Nintendo's eShop or the Nintendo Switch Online service to acquire the Nintendo Switch edition of the game.

The iOS mobile device version of the game (shown here on an iPad Pro) is available from the Apple App Store, while the Android-based version of the game (when it becomes available) can be acquired from the Google Play Store.

A continuous Internet connection is required to download and play any version of *Fortnite: Battle Royale*. If you're playing on a PC or Mac, or any mobile device, you'll also need a free Epic Games account. PlayStation 4 gamers require a PlayStation Network account, while a paid membership to Xbox Gold is required for Xbox One users.

Fortnite Resources

Pro gamers around the world have created YouTube channels, online forums, and blogs focused exclusively on *Fortnite: Battle Royale*. Plus, you can watch pro players compete online and describe their best strategies or check out the coverage about *Fortnite: Battle Royale* published by leading gaming websites and magazines.

On YouTube (www.youtube.com) or Twitch. TV (www.twitch.tv/directory/game/Fortnite), in the Search field, enter the search phrase "Fortnite: Battle Royale" to discover many game-related channels, live streams, and pre-recorded videos.

Be sure to check out these awesome online resources that will help you become a better *Fortnite: Battle Royale* player:

WEBSITE OR YOUTUBE CHANNEL NAME	DESCRIPTION	URL
Epic Games' *Fortnite* YouTube Channel	The official *Fortnite* YouTube channel.	www.youtube.com/user/epicfortnite
Epic Games' official *Fortnite* website	Learn all about *Fortnite: Battle Royale*, as well as the paid editions of *Fortnite*.	www.Fortnite.com
Epic Games' official Twitter feed for *Fortnite*	The official *Fortnite* Twitter feed.	https://twitter.com/fortnitegame (@fortnitegame)
FantasticalGamer	A popular YouTuber who publishes Fortnite tutorial videos.	www.youtube.com/user/FantasticalGamer
Fandom's *Fortnite* Wiki	Discover the latest news and strategies related to *Fortnite*.	http://fortnite.wikia.com/wiki/Fortnite_Wiki
Fortnite Insider	The *Fortnite* Insider website offers game-related news, tips, and strategy videos.	www.fortniteinsider.com
FortniteBattleRoyale.org	This is an independent website that offers video tutorials for *Fortnite: Battle Royale*. It's not affiliated with Epic Games.	http://fortnitebattleroyale.org
Fortnite Tracker Network (FTN)	Visit this independent website and enter your Epic Games account username, or the username for any of the more than 13 million other *Fortnite: Battle Royale* players, to view a detailed ranking for that gamer. See things like number of wins, wins percentage, number of kills, and overall ranking (based on game play mode). Click on the "Popular" option to see the successes of the most popular and highly ranked players in the world.	https://fortnitetracker.com
Game Informer Magazine's *Fortnite* Coverage	Discover articles, reviews, and news about Fortnite published by *Game Informer* magazine.	www.gameinformer.com/search/searchresults.aspx?q=Fortnite
Gamespot	Check out *Gamespot*'s ongoing news coverage of *Fortnite: Battle Royal*	www.gamespot.com/fortnite/news
Game Skinny Online Guides	A collection of topic-specific strategy guides related to *Fortnite*.	www.gameskinny.com/tag/fortnite-guides
IGN Entertainment's *Fortnite* Coverage	Check out all IGN's past and current coverage of *Fortnite*.	www.ign.com/wikis/fortnite

(Continued on next page)

Jason R. Rich's Website and Social Media Feeds	Share your *Fortnite* game play strategies with this book's author and learn about his other books.	www.JasonRich.com Twitter: @JasonRich7 Instagram: @JasonRich7
Microsoft's Xbox One *Fortnite* Website	Learn about and acquire *Fortnite: Battle Royale* if you're an Xbox One gamer.	www.microsoft.com/en-US/store/p/Fortnite-Battle-Royalee/BT5P2X999VH2
MMORPG.com	Read the latest information about *Fortnite: Battle Royale* on this website that covers multiplayer online gaming.	www.mmorpg.com/fortnite/news
MonsterDface YouTube and Twitch.tv Channels	Watch video tutorials and live game streams from an expert *Fortnite* player.	www.youtube.com/user/MonsterdfaceLive www.Twitch.tv/MonsterDface
Nomxs	A YouTube and Twitch TV channel hosted by online personality Simon Britton (Nomxs). It features *Fortnite* game streams.	https://youtu.be/np-8cmsUZmc www.twitch.tv/videos/259245155
Sony's PS4 *Fortnite* Website	Learn about and acquire *Fortnite* if you're a PS4 gamer.	www.playstation.com/en-us/games/fortnite-ps4
Turtle Beach Corp.	This is one of several companies that make awesome quality gaming headsets that work great with a PS4, Xbox One, Nintendo Switch, PC, or Mac. Being able to hear crystal-clear sound, plus hold conversations with fellow gamers, is essential when playing *Fortnite*. It also works well with any mobile device that has a headphone jack.	www.turtlebeach.com

Fortnite: Save the World

When you purchase the *Fortnite* game, this is a related, but totally separate, story-based game. It does, however, include full access to *Fortnite: Battle Royale*.

It's currently available for PC, Mac, Playstation 4, and Xbox One. By 2019, Epic Games is expected to make Fortnite: Save the World a free game as well on all popular gaming platforms, including the Nintendo Switch.

Fortress

Using resources (wood, stone, and/or metal), you have the ability to build simple or extremely elaborate fortresses during a match in order to protect your soldier, or from which you can launch potentially devastating attacks when you're armed with an explosive projectile weapon (such as a grenade launcher) or a long-range rifle (with or without a scope).

A simple fortress can be a single level, and simply include four walls around you, and maybe a roof. More elaborate fortresses can be many levels tall, and designed using your own creativity, based on the situation you're facing.

In addition to referring back to the "Building Techniques" section of this guide, be sure to spend time watching *Fortnite: Battle Royale*'s Spectator Mode (after you get eliminated from a match) or watch live streams and videos on YouTube or Twitch.tv that showcase highly experienced and top-ranked players building forts during the End Game. Watching other players will give you great ideas for fortress designs and help you determine the best times and locations to build elaborate fortresses.

Freefall

As soon as you depart the Battle Bus, your soldier will freefall toward the ground. During this time, control the movement and falling speed of your soldier. This will help you reach a desired landing location.

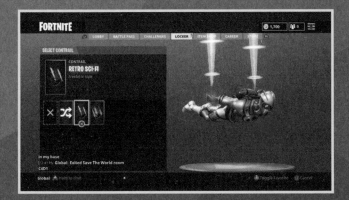

One of the character customizations you can add to your soldier is an animated freefall contrail. This is something you need to either unlock or purchase.

Once you've acquired one or more contrails, select the one you want from the Locker prior to a match. From the Locker, select and highlight the Contrail option (located to the right of the Glider option), and then choose from an unlocked contrail.

The contrail you choose is cosmetic only. It does not impact your soldier's rate of descent, or anything related to their freefall.

Anytime during freefall, activate your soldier's glider to dramatically slow down their rate of descent and give you very precise control over their directional movements while traveling toward the ground. As your soldier is falling toward the island, you can activate and deactivate the glider as often as you wish. However, if you wait too long to deploy the glider, it will automatically activate as your soldier gets close to the ground—ensuring a safe landing.

Game Play Modes

The core *Fortnite: Battle Royale* game play modes include:

- **Solo**—One player competes against up to 99 opponents.
- **Duo**—A player and one teammate compete against up to 98 opponents. You can play with a friend or be matched up with a stranger by the game.
- **Squads**—A team of up to four players compete against all other opponents (out of a total of 100 players per match). You can play with friends or be matched up with up to three strangers by the game.

Periodically Epic Games introduces additional game play modes and competitions that are available for a limited time. As you can see from this Choose Game Mode menu, Solid Gold V2 (Squads) and 50 v 50 V2 (Squads) modes are offered here. Notice the Limited Time Only! banner displayed when one of these two modes was selected.

Game Update (Patch)

Every week or two, Epic Games releases a game update (also referred to as a "patch"). A game update will often introduce a new game play mode, new weapons, new loot items, new challenges, or make relatively small tweaks to the game.

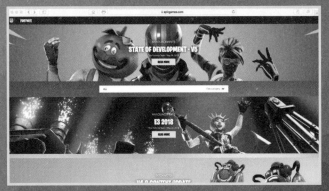

When a new update is available, you'll need to download and install it on your gaming system in order to continue playing *Fortnite: Battle Royale*. A pop-up window will appear that explains some of the new gaming features and changes. This information is also published online, at: www.epicgames.com/fortnite/en-US/news.

Gamer's Headset

Sound is an extremely important element of the *Fortnite: Battle Royale* game play experience. It's essential that you be able to hear the sounds made by your opponents and be able to determine when your soldier is making too much noise as a result of their actions.

From the Settings menu, select the Audio submenu (shown), and consider turning up the Sound FX Volume option, so you'll be able to clearly hear all the important sound effects being generated. At the same time, feel free to turn down the Music volume and/or Voice Chat volume.

The best way to experience the audio incorporated into the game, and to be able to communicate verbally with your squad members (if applicable) is to use a gamer's headset anytime you're playing *Fortnite: Battle Royale*.

Shown here is a popular headset from Turtle Beach Corp. (www.turtlebeach.com), although many companies make stereo headsets with a built-in microphone that are compatible with all of the popular gaming platforms.

Glider

The glider is the device that's used to end a soldier's freefall and help him/her land safely on the island, while allowing the gamer precise control over the landing location. During freefall, you're able to activate and deactivate the glider as often as you like, but it automatically deploys during the final moments of freefall.

Just as many different and optional outfits are available for soldiers, each offers an optional glider designer, which can be purchased or unlocked separately. Once you've unlocked multiple glider designs, choose the one you want to use before any match by accessing the Locker.

Each of the glider designs looks drastically different, although they all work exactly the same way. The difference between glider designs is only their appearance.

Graphic Emote

This is one of three types of emotes available. Refer to the listing for "Emotes" for more information. When a graphic emote is used, a soldier throws a graphic icon into the air for everyone in the immediate area to see.

Each icon must be unlocked or acquired separately. Choose which graphic emotes you want accessible from the Locker. During a match, access this Emotes menu to display a desired emote.

Greasy Grove

Fast food restaurants, plus a few stores and several homes are what you'll encounter in this region of the island, which can be found at map coordinates C7.

Explore the buildings to find loot and potentially hide from enemies. You can also place traps or remote explosives within the buildings to surprise enemies with a painful blast. If you don't yet have a trap, one might be for sale from the Vending Machine.

It's within the attics and basements (if applicable) of the homes that you'll find chests and other useful weapons, ammo, and loot. Land on a roof and smash your way down; enter a home through a door and work your way up; or from the outside, build a ramp to the top of the roof and smash your way down. Don't forget to search the stores as well (shown here).

Located a short distance from Greasy Grove is a sports complex that's not labeled on the map. You'll find it near coordinates C5. There's an indoor swimming pool here. Explore it, and you'll likely find at least one chest, as well as plenty of other weapons, ammo, and loot.

The indoor soccer field, and the rooms and areas that surround it, are also chock full of useful loot to collect.

Grenade Launcher

This is one of the more powerful projectile and explosive weapons available. From a distance, you can accurately aim at a target and fire this weapon. Upon impact, it'll explode. A direct hit to a building or structure will cause serious damage or result in it collapsing. A direct hit to an enemy soldier will cause their immediate demise. Most gamers save their grenade launcher until the End Game portion of a match, but this weapon can be used anytime to damage or pummel any structure, building, or enemy.

Grenades

These are weapons that get tossed at an enemy or target location. They explode on impact. The closer an enemy is to the explosion, the more damage it will cause. Grenades can also be used to destroy buildings or structures. A soldier can collect and carry multiple grenades within a single backpack slot.

If your soldier is too close to the explosion once they've tossed a grenade, the damage could be devastating! A grenade can bounce off of a wall or object and be repelled back toward the thrower, so be careful.

H

Haunted Hills

The churches, crypts, and graveyard in this relatively small region (located at map coordinates B3) provide an ideal setting for shootouts. There's also great scavenging to be done here for chests, weapons, ammo, loot, and stone.

Be sure to explore the basement and tower within each of the churches.

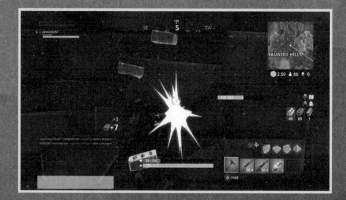

Inside the churches, smash through the stone walls to reveal hidden crypts and rooms that typically contain a chest or loot.

Inside the smaller stone crypts, you'll often discover loot. These also provide a temporary shelter from enemy gunfire if you go inside and block the entrance by building a wall.

Each church typically contains at least one or two chests. From the higher levels of a church, choose a sniping location, crouch down (to achieve better aim), and then use a shotgun, long-range rifle, or sniper rifle (with a scope) to target enemy soldiers below.

Health Points (HP)

Displayed near the bottom-center of the screen (on most gaming platforms) is a soldier's Health meter (displayed in green). The Shield meter is displayed directly above the Health meter (in blue). The Health meter displays the number of

Health Points (HP) your soldier has remaining. This can be between zero and 100. When the Health meter (or the number of Health Points possessed) reaches zero, your soldier is immediately eliminated from the match.

Each time your soldier receives an injury, some of their HP gets depleted. This can be from a bullet wound, a fall, or the result of an explosion, for example.

Throughout a match, there are multiple ways to boost your soldier's HP. For example, you can consume an Apple, Chug Jug, or Slurp Juice. You can also utilize a Cozy Campfire, Bandages, or Med Kit. These are types of loot you'll discover throughout the island, or that in some cases can be acquired from chests, Supply Drops, or Vending Machines, for example.

Hidden Rooms

Many homes, buildings, and structures found on the island contain hidden rooms. These are particularly common in the attics or basements of homes, or within the churches (found in Haunted Hills).

You'll often need to use the pickaxe to smash through a wall, floor, or ceiling in order to discover and access a hidden room. If there's a chest within a hidden room, as you approach a wall that will lead to that room, you'll hear the familiar sound generated by a chest when you're close to it, even if you can't see it.

Hop Rocks

During Season 4, when the island was bombarded by comets, Hop Rocks appeared within many of the craters. When consumed, for about 30 seconds, a soldier is able to jump higher, and leap farther, and will not be injured when jumping or falling from high up.

Once the Hop Rock is consumed, a soldier will begin to glow. Whether or not the craters will remain once Season 4 comes to an end is anyone's guess. If the craters are removed from the game in Season 5 or later, chances are Hop Rocks will become a thing of the past as well.

Impulse Grenades

This type of grenade inflicts damage to enemies, plus throws them into the air, away from the point of impact. A soldier can collect and carry multiple Impulse Grenades in a single backpack slot. This type of weapon gets tossed at an enemy.

Island

The island is where every match takes place. On the island are more than 20 different (labeled) points of interest, in addition to an ever-growing number of areas that are not labeled on the map. Throughout a match, a soldier can travel anywhere on the map. However, it's best to avoid the deadly storm that forms and expands throughout the island once a match begins.

Island Map

While in the pre-deployment area, during freefall, or anytime when on the island, access the island map.

During Season 4, this is what the map looked like immediately after arriving on the island, before the storm materialized. Many of the island's points of interest are clearly labeled, although some smaller locations are not labeled. These unlabeled areas often offer multiple chests and an abundance of weapons, ammo, and loot to gather. To make it easier to identify specific locations on the map, whether or not they're labeled, map coordinates are used. See the "Map Coordinates" listing for more information.

The island map displays your current location (as a white, triangle-shaped icon). The uninhabitable area of the island, due to the storm, is displayed in pink. The inner white circle previews where the storm will be expanding to next.

Item Shop

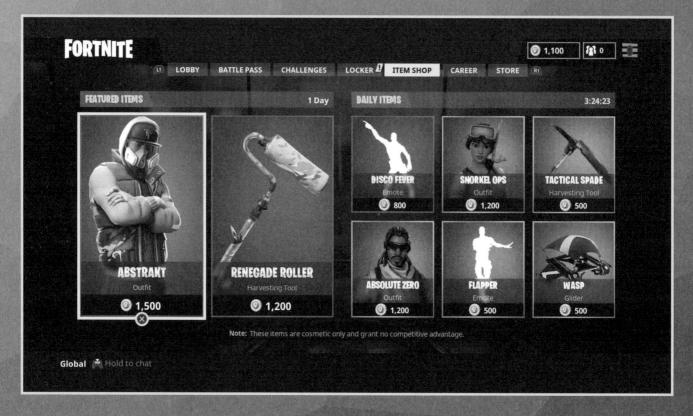

Every day, a new selection of limited edition items, including outfits, pickaxe designs, glider designs, and emotes are available for purchase from the Item Shop. It's accessible from the Lobby. One item can be purchased at a time using V-Bucks (which cost real money to acquire). The items sold from the Item Shop are typically only available for a single day, although some are re-introduced multiple times.

Jetpack

This was a limited time loot item introduced during Season 4, although it could make a comeback at any time. If you find a Jetpack, strap it on, and for a short time, fly at a fast speed while controlling your movement. Use it to reach far-off areas quickly, escape being caught in the storm, rush an opponent, or initiate an attack from midair. Here, this gamer was using a Jetpack to fly above their soldier's fort to get a better look around during the End Game.

Junk Junction

Found between map coordinates B1.5 and C1.5, old cars are piled up everywhere within Junk Junction. You'll often find items to collect on top of car piles. On the ground, between the piles, is a maze-like area to explore.

Outside of Junk Junction (near map coordinates B1), be sure to explore this llama-shaped tower

to find several chests and other weapons. If possible, after leaving the Battle Bus, land on top of this tower and smash your way down.

As you can see here, the ground level of Junk Junction is a maze-like area. It's safer to explore Junk Junction from higher levels as opposed to ground level, especially if there are enemies lurking around the area. Either climb to the top of junk piles and jump between them, or build bridges that'll help you stay on the high ground.

Consider placing a trap or remote explosive at ground level near the car piles. As an enemy soldier explores the maze-like area, you can defeat them with a surprise explosion while you're a safe distance away.

Be sure to explore the buildings in the Junk Junction area, as well as the structures you'll discover just outside of Junk Junction, near map coordinates C1.

Landing Location

After departing from the Battle Bus and entering into freefall, this is the location on the island you choose to land. Some players opt to land smack in the middle of a popular point of interest and are willing to confront enemy soldiers right from the start. Others choose to land at a more remote, less populated, or even deserted area of the island, which gives them more time to build an arsenal and gather resources before having to engage in firefights or battle enemies.

Launch Pad

This item can be collected and used to quickly catapult your soldier into the air, activate their glider, and then precisely transport them to a different location. It is a rare item. It's useful for escaping the storm if you get stuck deep in uninhabitable territory. A Launch Pad is also useful to rush a distant opponent to launch a close-range attack.

To use a Launch Pad, it must be placed on a flat surface. Once it's placed on the ground, have your soldier step on the platform to activate it.

Your soldier will be catapulted into the air upon stepping on the Launch Pad.

Once the soldier's glider deploys, steer it the same way as you did when your soldier first approached the island upon leaving the Battle Bus.

Lobby

This is the main screen from which you're able to choose a game play mode, enter into a match, view details about your soldier (including his/her experience level), see the current challenges, read bulletins from Epic Games, plus access the Battle Pass, Challenges, Locker, Item Shop, Career, or Store area, as well as the Settings menu.

Location Map

Continuously displayed on the screen during a match is a tiny location map. It's also referred to as the "mini map." Here it's shown in the top-right corner of the screen. Depending on which gaming system you're using, the location of this map will vary.

The location map shows your current position on the island. Look for the white triangle icon. If you get caught in the storm, or you're outside of where the safe area will be once the storm expands, follow the white line to safety. If you're near the edge of the circle, the white line of the circle's perimeter is also displayed. Areas shown in pink are uninhabitable, due to the storm.

Locker

This is the virtual storage space where all of the character customization items you purchase, unlock, or acquire get stored when they're not being used. Access the Locker before a match to customize the appearance of your soldier using the items currently available to you.

The Locker is divided into three sections. On the right, your character's current appearance is displayed. Under the Account and Equipment heading, individual sections of the Locker allow you to choose your banner, outfit, back bling design, pickaxe design, contrail design, and loading screen design. Below these options, under the Emotes heading, choose six different types of emotes (including graphic emotes, dance moves, and spray paint tags) that you want to be able to utilize during a match.

Once you acquire a new item from the Item Shop, or unlock a new item, it will appear automatically within the appropriate section of your Locker. If a small yellow banner displaying a number appears in the top-right corner of a Locker section, this means that new items are available. Only items that you've unlocked, acquired, or earned will be displayed within the Locker.

Lonely Lodge

Located at map coordinates J5, Lonely Lodge is where you'll find a lodge, a collection of cabins, parked RVs, and a tall observation tower.

The most exciting place to explore near this point of interest is this massive waterfront mansion (found at map coordinates J5).

As you approach the front door of the mansion, use the pickaxe to smash into the ground. You'll discover the entrance to a hidden basement. It contains some type of high-tech control center that's filled with awesome items to collect. There are several chests to be found here.

Within Lonely Lodge, be sure to explore the main lodge. You'll find chests and other goodies inside.

The tallest structure in the area is this wooden observation tower. Near the top in particular, you'll find some great loot. If you climb to the top, don't fall or jump off, or you'll perish. However, if you engage an enemy soldier in a fight near the top of this tower, try to force them to jump or fall over the edge.

Many of the small cabins in the area contain weapons, ammo, and loot. You can easily booby trap one or more of these cabins with traps or remote explosives, or hide inside, close the door behind you, crouch down, draw your weapon, and wait for an enemy soldier to enter. When they do, ambush them!

Loot

Many types of loot are available, although some are rarer and harder to come by than others. Some of the more popular loot items you may discover and be able to collect and carry in your backpack, and then use during a match (at your discretion), include Bandages, Boogie Bombs, Bushes, Cozy Campfires, Chug Jugs, Clingers, Grenades, Impulse Grenades, Jetpacks, Launch Pads, Small Shield Potions, Med Kits, Port-A-Forts, Remote Explosives, Shield Potions, Slurp Juice, and Traps. See the listings in this guide for each type of loot to learn more about what each does and how it's used.

Some loot items, like Apples and Hop Rocks, must be consumed as soon as they're found. They can't be picked up and carried in your backpack to be used at a later time. Consuming or using loot that replenishes your health and/or shields take time to use, so plan accordingly and make sure you're in a safe or secluded space.

One of the more important decisions you'll need to make during a match is choosing which type(s) of loot you want to carry in your backpack at any given time, so those items are readily available to you. Remember, you only have six backpack slots, and one of those is always taken by your pickaxe. At least one or

two of the remaining slots should be used to carry weapons, such as some type of gun.

Within a single backpack slot, you can hold multiples of the same loot items. For example, you can carry as many grenades as you can find or collect during a match, and then use one at a time, when they're needed.

Loot Lake

In the middle of the lake (found at map coordinates E4), there's an island that contains a house. Inside, you'll discover chests and other useful items to collect. Then, make your way to the rowboat in the center of the lake, as well as the buildings (located near docks) on the opposite side of the lake.

Instead of walking through the lake to cross it (which is a slow process that leaves you out in the open and exposed to potential enemy attacks), build a bridge over the water. Once you start crossing the water on foot, however, you can't start building a bridge in the middle of the water. The bridge needs to begin on land.

If you attempt to reach the rowboat in the lake, empty the chest quickly, and be prepared to evade enemy fire. If you have a sniper rifle (or rifle with a scope), stay on land and shoot at enemy soldiers that attempt to reach the rowboat.

The house on the island is chock full of items worth collecting, so search carefully, but be prepared to encounter enemy soldiers.

The two buildings located near the docks are both worth searching, although you're more apt to find chests and useful loot in the larger of the buildings. As you approach either building, watch out for snipers.

Additional structures have been added around Loot Lake, many of which contain some awesomely useful loot. Consider traveling around the lake (instead of crossing it) to explore the structures you encounter. The hut with a dock that's on the lake (right), the wooden tower (middle), and a multi-level house (left) are all close together, near map coordinates E4.

Loot Llama

While Supply Drops happen randomly throughout each match, they tend to be rare. An even rarer occurrence, however, is finding a Loot Llama. This is a llama-shaped statue (that looks like a colorful piñata). It contains a random collection of often rare loot, weapons, ammo, and/or resource icons (similar to a Supply Drop or chest).

Should you happen to stumble upon a Loot Llama, approach it with caution, in case enemies are nearby waiting to attack you. Consider quickly building four walls (and a ceiling) around you and the Loot Llama for protection before opening it.

Opening a Loot Llama takes about eight seconds. You then need time to safely pick and choose which items you want to grab. It'll often be necessary to take time to reorganize your backpack's inventory to accommodate the new, powerful, and rare weapons, ammo, and loot you find. This Loot Llama offered 500 wood, 500 stone, and 500 metal, along with a trap, a selection of ammo, and Clingers.

Watch out for flashing lights when you spot a Loot Llama. Instead of opening a Loot Llama, some gamers transform it into a weapon by attaching remote explosives to it. Then, as soon as someone else approaches, the explosives get detonated, and the approaching soldier is terminated with a bang. If you see the flashing lights of a remote explosive, stay clear and don't approach.

However, if you find yourself with a good arsenal and you don't need anything else, consider setting your own trap when you encounter a Loot Llama by attaching remote explosives to it. Then hide somewhere nearby and wait for an enemy to approach.

Lucky Landing

Found between map coordinates F10 and G10, the buildings in and around this point of interest all have an Asian influence. Within the building that contains the giant pink tree, you're apt to find rare and powerful weapons. However, be sure to explore all of the buildings, bridges, and towers in this region.

This bridge that leads to Lucky Landing offers weapons, ammo, and loot to collect, both within the bridge and below it.

There's a chest to be found in the main room of this Asian temple.

Go to the top floor of this office building. In addition to finding items within the building, the large window on the top floor offers a great view of the area, from which you can use any long-range weapon to shoot at enemy soldiers below. Targeting enemies on the ground is easier with a rifle that contains a scope, but any rifle or shotgun, for example, should do

the trick. As always, a head shot causes much more damage than a body shot. Using a projectile explosive, such as a rocket launcher or grenade launcher, will destroy the structure you shoot at and likely defeat anyone inside.

Don't forget to look inside the buildings, including behind the counters in stores and restaurants, to find chests. Check the shelves for ammo boxes. On the floor of almost every building in this area, you'll discover weapons, ammo, or loot waiting to be grabbed. In the building with the pink tree in the center, weapons can often be found on the ground in every corner of the structure if you're the first person to get there.

MAG (Magazine) Capacity

When it comes to evaluating the power and capabilities of a weapon, MAG Capacity represents the total number of ammunition rounds (or bullets) the weapon can hold at once, before it needs to be reloaded. Reloading a weapon takes valuable time, during which your soldier will be vulnerable to attack.

Shotguns have a small MAG Capacity but each round of ammunition packs a wallop when you make a direct hit. Machine guns and certain other weapons have a much larger MAG Capacity, but each individual bullet typically causes less damage when a direct hit is made.

Map Coordinates

As you can see here, the full island map is divided into quadrants (boxes). Displayed along the top margin of the map (from left to right) are the letters "A" through "J." Along the left margin of the map, from top to bottom, are the numbers "1" through "10." Using these letters and numbers, you can easily identify any location or quadrant on the map.

While viewing the island map, it's possible to zoom in and scroll around in order to view a particular area of the island in more detail. By zooming in on areas of the map, you can more closely see unlabeled points of interest, like the motel between map coordinates D2 and E2. (Here, it's near the top-center of the screen.)

Match

A match begins the moment up to 100 soldiers land on the island, and ends when only one soldier remains alive and most of the island has become uninhabitable due to the expansion of the storm. The average match lasts about 15 minutes, but its duration has a lot to do with the skill of the players and how quickly eliminations happen. When a soldier's Health meter is depleted, they're eliminated from the match.

Med Kits

Whether it's the result of a gunshot wound, getting caught in an explosion, or taking a fall, it's extremely likely that during a match, your soldier will take damage, and at least some of their Health Points (HP) will be depleted.

Consuming a Med Kit restores your health to 100 percent. It takes 10 seconds to use a Med Kit, during which time your solider is vulnerable to attack.

One way to replenish your soldier's Health Points is to use a Med Kit. These can be found in chests and Supply Drops or acquired from Vending Machines or by defeating an enemy and taking their loot. Occasionally, you'll spot a Med Kit lying on the ground waiting to be collected. Within your backpack, you're able to store multiple Med Kits in a single slot, and then use them, one at a time, when they're needed.

Metal

One of the three types of resources you'll need to collect or harvest during a match is metal. Then, when it comes to building, using metal is the strongest material available to you. It can withstand the most damage before its destroyed. As a result, building a protective wall or fort from metal gives you the most protection.

Metal can be harvested using your pickaxe to smash anything made of metal that you discover on the island. This includes cars, trucks, metal fencing, farm silos, machinery, or kitchen appliances found in homes, for example. Anytime you harvest metal, it makes a lot of noise and can easily attract enemy soldiers to your location.

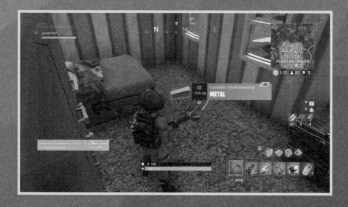

Additional ways to collect metal include defeating enemy soldiers and collecting their resources or finding and grabbing metal icons (shown here) that are scattered throughout the island. Resource icons can sometimes be found within chests too.

Miniguns

This is just one of the many types of weapons to be found, collected, and used on the island. Miniguns can be used from any range and are useful for spraying a wall or structure with bullets in order to destroy it. Of course, this type of weapon can cause some major damage when bullets from it hit enemy soldiers.

Moisty Mire

Located at map coordinates I9, this region contains lots of trees that make up a dense forest. Near the outskirts of Moisty Mire is an abandoned prison.

Within the prison area, search the guard towers, and then make your way to the individual prison cells. Smash through walls in the prison cells and you'll discover offices, guard rooms, and other areas you can't otherwise reach.

Just outside the prison, you'll encounter a bunch of vehicles. Here, two of them contain chests.

Also located in this area is a movie set. Explore this area, where you'll find several buildings, a wooden observation tower, a swamp that contains a rowboat, and other interesting places to visit. Whenever you're out in the open and vulnerable to attack, proceed with caution and be ready to take cover.

The wooden observation tower contains a chest. This is also a good location from which you can shoot at enemies from above. According to rumors circulating in June 2018, at the start of Season 5, Moisty Mire will be getting a facelift, so expect to see some major changes here in the future.

Motel

You won't see this labeled on the island map, but located between map coordinates D2 and E2, you'll discover this rundown motel. Many of the structures in this area, including several former guestrooms, contain multiple items to collect.

Build a ramp to the loft area within this former guestroom, and you'll discover one of the several chests in this area. You can see the glow from the chest near the top-center of this screen. This motel is a great place to visit if you want to quickly build up your arsenal.

Muscle Memory

The concept of establishing and using your muscle memory applies when playing almost any computer or video game. The goal is to practice playing, and repeat the same actions so often, that it becomes second nature to you. In other words, you train yourself to know exactly what to press on the wireless controller, keyboard/mouse, or touchscreen, and know exactly when to do it, so you don't need to waste time thinking about it.

In terms of playing *Fortnite: Battle Royale*, with practice, you'll want to train your muscle memory to help you accomplish common tasks, including:

- Quickly switching between and selecting weapons within your backpack.
- Aiming your selected weapon and firing accurately at your targets.
- Switching between building, resource collection/harvesting, and fighting mode.
- Quickly building structures and being able to switch between building pieces and building materials.
- Accessing the island map, Emotes menu, and Quick Chat menu during a match.

Outfit

Every day Epic Games releases new outfits you can purchase for your soldier. Throughout this guide, many different (optional) outfits and soldier customizations are shown.

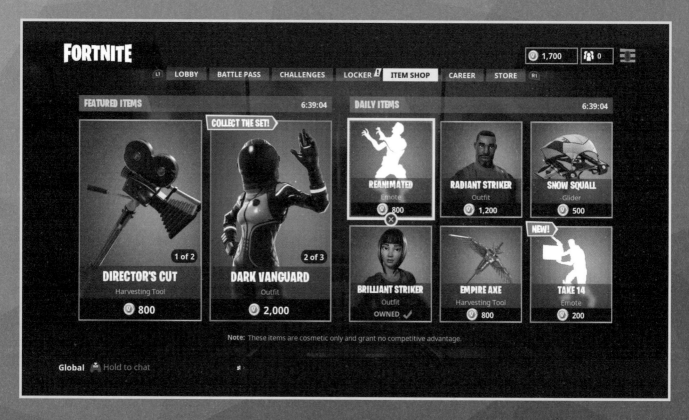

Outfits are available from the Item Shop. In addition, you're able to unlock outfits by accomplishing Battle Pass-related goals or by acquiring free downloadable items from promotional partners. (See the listing for "Twitch Prime Packs.") On this particular day, the featured outfit was Dark Vanguard, and its cost was 2,000 V-Bucks.

Patch Notes

Every time Epic Games releases a game up-date for *Fortnite: Battle Royale*, on its website you'll find an "Announcements" and "Patch Notes" section. These sections of the website explain what's new and what's been tweaked or changed within the game.

To read the latest Patch Notes, visit: www.epicgames.com/fortnite/en-US/news.

Whenever something new and exciting is add-ed, a pop-up New Updates message appears when you launch *Fortnite: Battle Royale*.

Pickaxe

The pickaxe is a soldier's primary tool. It's available from the moment a soldier steps foot on the island, and when it's not in use, it gets stored within a soldier's backpack. It can't be dropped or replaced.

Use the pickaxe to harvest resources, smash apart or break through objects, and as a close-range weapon. Every outfit that Epic Games releases has an optional and matching pickaxe design. All pickaxes work exactly the same way.

From the Locker, you're able to choose the ap-pearance of your pickaxe, based on the designs you've purchased, unlocked, or acquired. Each day, at least one or two new pickaxe designs are offered for sale from the Item Shop.

Pistols

There are many types of handheld pistols available on the island. These tend to be com-mon and useful close-range weapons. They are far less powerful and less versatile, how-ever, than other types of weapons, such as shotguns.

Early in a match, grab a pistol and make it part of your arsenal, but this should be one of the first items to replace in your full back-pack, when more powerful weapons (that can also be used for close-range combat) become available. If you have a choice between a shotgun or a pistol, go with the shotgun.

Pleasant Park

In addition to Snobby Shores, this is an area of the island that contains a bunch of single-family homes. Found at map coordinates C3, there's also a park and sports field within this point of interest.

This is a popular area, so if you're not the first person to reach the center of the soccer field or the structure in the center of the area to open the chests, avoid these open areas, or you'll get shot. It's easy to snipe someone in the open areas by staking a location on the top floor or roof of a nearby home.

The structure in the center of town often contains a chest, as well as a centralized location from which you can shoot at enemies in all directions around you. Build a mini-fort above the structure in the center of town, and you'll have a 360-degree view of the area. Using a shotgun, sniper rifle, or any rifle with a scope, you'll be able to pick off enemy soldiers with relative ease, without having to move around too much.

As with any home on the island, the best approach is to land on the roof (or from the outside, build a ramp to the roof), and then smash your way down into the attic using your pickaxe. Inside the homes, you'll likely encounter enemy soldiers, so listen carefully for their footsteps and movements, especially before you open the door to a room or climb up or down stairs.

Point of Interest

A point of interest is a location on the island map that is labeled, and that tends to be popular. Each point of interest features a different type of terrain, offers a different selection of buildings and structures to explore, and contains an assortment of chests, weapons, ammo, loot, and resources that can be collected.

During Season 4, the island map contained 20 labeled points of interest on the map, along with several areas that were popular, but not labeled. Risky Reels was one of the new points of interest added.

As each new season kicks off, you'll discover alterations to the island map. For example, you might discover a new point of interest, or notice that a point of interest has been dramatically altered.

Keep in mind, any time a new point of interest is added to the island map, it becomes an extremely popular landing spot, because everyone wants to check it out. As a result, as soon as you land there, you'll encounter many enemy soldiers. To survive, you must be one of the first to land, and then find and grab a weapon. Otherwise, you'll get shot within moments after landing, while you're still unarmed.

When you want to visit a very popular point of interest, consider landing in the outskirts of that area. Collect weapons, ammo, loot, and resources, and then go into that area fully armed and ready to fight. While you'll likely survive longer, you'll notice that as a latecomer to the area during a match, the chests are likely to have been opened, and the available weapons, ammo, and loot will have been collected. By defeating enemies, however, you can grab everything they've collected.

The first few times you visit a new and popular point of interest, take the time to discover the location of chests, as well as where other weapons and items will likely be found in the future. Once you get to know the area, when you return in future matches, you'll know

exactly where to go to find the best loot, and where to go to stay safe.

Port-A-Fort

This is a loot item that's rare. Once found, however, it can be picked up and carried within your backpack until it's needed.

Once activated, a multi-level metal fort is instantly built. This fortress requires no resources to build. Use it to protect yourself from an incoming attack, or for additional protection as you use long-range or projectile weapons to launch an attack on others. Inside the fort are tires you can bounce on in order to reach the top of the fort quickly. From the top, if you look out over the edge, you'll get a 360-degree view of the surrounding area. Move down a bit, but stay near the top (shown on the previous page), and your soldier will be protected.

Pre-Deployment Area

A Port-a-Fort is tall and sturdy. Consider using it during an End Game, or anytime when you're anticipating a powerful incoming attack.

Prior to boarding the Battle Bus, this is the holding area where you'll wait until all of the players have joined the match. Any weapons or resources you find and collect in this area will be taken away when you board the Battle Bus. Feel free to explore this area, practice your dance moves, or use your other emotes. You can't be harmed in the pre-deployment area, so don't worry about being shot at, or getting smacked by an enemy's pickaxe.

Quick Builder Controller Layout

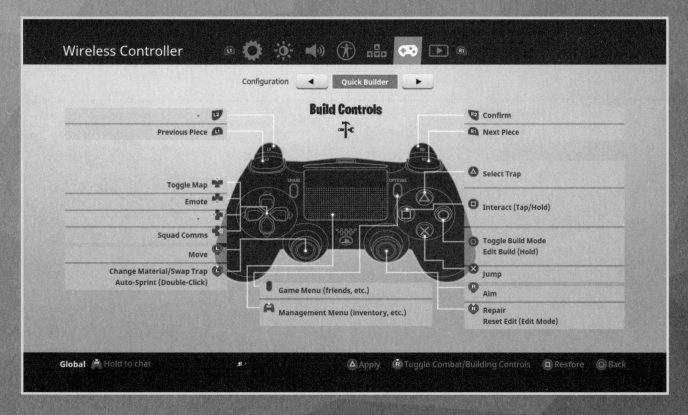

This particular controller layout (shown on the PS4) makes the commonly used game features associated with building more readily accessible. If you're a noob, initially stick with the Old School ("Standard") controller layout, because it makes the commonly used features for fighting, resource gathering, and building all easily accessible. Once you gain experience playing *Fortnite: Battle Royale*, and you discover your personal strategy focuses heavily on building, then consider switching to the Quick Builder or Pro Builder controller layout.

Reload Time

All of the different types of guns available within the game have a MAG Capacity, which determines how many bullets (or how much ammo) the weapon can hold. Once you use this ammo, assuming you have collected additional ammo, you'll need to reload the weapon. The reload time determines how long it takes to reload an empty weapon.

During the reload time, you can't shoot, and you're basically defenseless. Seriously consider hiding behind an object for added protection while reloading. Weapons with a slow reload time tend to use the most powerful bullets or ammo. Thus, one direct hit will cause a lot of damage. However, if your aim isn't too good, each round of ammo you use will result in little or no damage to your enemy. Then, when it comes time to reload, you'll be vulnerable to an incoming attack.

Until you've become a pro at aiming weapons, stick with weapon choices that have a large MAG Capacity and a quick reload time. Then, once you've perfected your aiming skills, consider using a weapon with more powerful ammo, but that has a slower reload time. One or two direct hits or headshots from a weapon with a slow reload time will defeat an enemy, so the reload time won't be an issue.

Remote Explosives

A soldier can carry up to 10 of these explosives at once. Activate it by attaching it to an object, wall, or structure, for example, and then detonate it remotely from any distance away.

After setting up a remote explosive, lure your adversary to its location before detonating it. Just make sure your soldier is far enough away to avoid the explosion. Watch for the blue light to know it's active.

Resources

Wood, stone, and metal are the three resources you'll want to collect and utilize during each match. Resources can be used for building, but they can also be used to purchase items from Vending Machines that are scattered throughout the island.

Scattered throughout the island are Wood, Stone, or Metal icons. Grab these to collect a bundle of that resource. Also, anytime you defeat an enemy soldier during a match, in addition to collecting their weapons, ammo, and loot, you can also grab their resources.

As you prepare for the End Game portion of a match, when you'll need to build at least one tall and sturdy fort, you'll ideally want to have at least 1,000 to 1,500 wood, stone, and/or metal resources at your disposal. The more resources you have, the better.

Retail Row

Found at map coordinates H5.5, this area contains a handful of shops, restaurants, a water tower, plus a few homes, most of which surround street parking areas. One of the unique things about this region is that chests are not always found in the same place.

You'll often discover a chest at the top of the water tower.

From the roof of this home, located near the end of Retail Row, smash your way downward. This home is missing a piece of its roof. If you look carefully, you'll spot a chest from above. If you know an enemy is hiding within a house or structure and you have explosive weapons at your disposal (such as a grenade launcher or remote explosive), blow up or destroy that house or structure. The enemy will likely perish.

Most of the stores and restaurants have weapons, ammo, and loot lying out in the open, on the ground, waiting to be collected. However, look for hidden rooms and areas where additional items, including chests, may also be available.

In the market, walk through the loading dock door, and then climb up on boxes and shelves. Near the ceilings, you'll find a chest.

Risky Reels

Found at map coordinates H2, the Risky Reels point of interest was added to the island in conjunction with Season 4. Here, you'll find a drive-in movie theater. In the parking lot are a bunch of abandoned cars and trucks.

Check the backs of trucks for chests and loot, and then explore the area near the movie screen, as well as the nearby buildings. Smash the cars and trucks to collect metal. (But plan on making a lot of noise as you do this.)

Go inside the concession stand (snack shop). A chest can be found inside the bathroom stalls. Watch for its golden glow.

Within the large shed containing picnic tables, you'll often find a chest, as well as other weapons and loot lying out in the open.

There's an old house located near the drive-in theater. Explore it like you would any house, and you'll likely find plenty of weapons, ammo, and loot, not to mention a chest in the attic.

Rock Formations

Scattered throughout the island are rock formations. Hide behind large rock formations for protection. Using your pickaxe, smash apart the rocks to harvest stone.

Rocket Launchers

Use a rocket launcher as a long-range and explosive projectile weapon to destroy buildings and structures (and defeat anyone who's hiding within them). One direct hit from a rocket launcher will defeat any enemy, regardless of how far away they are.

During the End Game portion of a match, rocket launchers are extremely useful weapons. They allow you to stay in the safety and comfort of your fortress and launch devastating attacks on enemy forts and soldiers from a distance.

For a rocket launcher to be useful, you must have an ample supply of ammo for it. Throughout a match, collect appropriate ammo, even if you're not yet holding a rocket launcher. You'll find this ammo out in the open, lying on the ground, within chests, and within ammo boxes. It can also be acquired from defeated enemies.

Roof Landing

Since the best weapons, ammo, and loot can often be found in the attics of homes and mansions, as well as on the top level of towers, buildings, and other tall structures (like silos, clock towers, and water towers), consider landing on the roof of a building or structure after exiting the Battle Bus. Then, from the roof, use your pickaxe to smash your way downward.

As you're about to land on a roof, if you notice an enemy soldier has already landed there, you have three choices. First, you can land near the enemy and use your pickaxe to attack them. Victory will require multiple direct hits. Second, if you see a weapon nearby, be the first to grab it, and then shoot the other soldier (before he has a chance to grab that weapon). Third, choose an alternate landing site.

When you land on a roof, knowing that there's a chest in the attic to top floor directly below, you'll need to smash through the roof to reach it. If another soldier chooses to land on the same roof, the soldier who breaks through the roof, reaches the chest, and grabs the first weapon will likely shoot and defeat the other.

Run

In addition to walking and tiptoeing, running is one of the main ways your soldier can move around on the island. It also tends to be the fastest, unless you happen to have a Launch Pad or Jetpack at your disposal.

To keep running, press and hold down the Run button on your controller (or mouse/keyboard). There's also an optional Run Lock option, so your soldier will keep running without you having to hold down the Run button.

Rush Opponent

Rushing an opponent means you quickly move toward them to launch a close-range attack. For example, during the End Game portion of a match, if you and an adversary are both safe within your respective fortresses, and you decide to leave your fortress and run toward the enemy fortress to attack it, this is referred to as rushing your opponent.

Salty Springs

Found at map coordinates F7, here you'll discover a group of single-family homes and a gas station that are clustered together. Be sure to search the homes but be on the lookout for enemy soldiers who may be lurking within them.

As always, if you're about to search a home, mansion, or building, and you notice the front or back door is already open, this means someone else has gotten there before you (possibly multiple people) and they could still be inside.

The homes in Salty Springs and throughout the island may all look different from the outside, but inside, most contain several floors, each with a handful of rooms.

This stone structure is definitely worth visiting, especially if you need to find and grab some weapons. The stone structure is also heavily fortified, so it makes a good hiding place if you need one.

Seasons

Every three to four months, Epic Games introduces a new Season to *Fortnite: Battle Royale*. This includes a significant game update which typically includes new weapons, loot items, points of interest, challenges, and a new Battle Pass. At the start of each new Season, your soldier's Experience Level returns to 1, but you keep all of your outfits and items.

Settings Menu

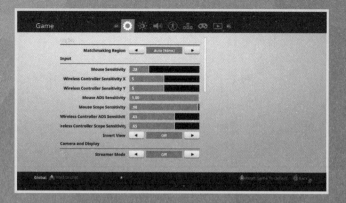

Access the Settings menu to make adjustments to a handful of game play features. Especially if you're new to playing *Fortnite*, don't waste time tinkering with these options. As you become better acquainted with the game, consider making small adjustments to the features that you think will make you more competitive. For example, make sure Auto Equip Better Items, Aim Assist, Turbo Building, and Auto Material Change are turned on.

Turning on Auto Pick Up Weapons can save you valuable seconds when you come across new weapons that you want to grab. When turned on, you simply need to run over a weapon to grab it. Keep in mind, if your backpack is full and your soldier grabs a new weapon, whichever weapon he/she was holding and that was selected will be dropped. The new one will be picked up automatically.

Shield Meter

Throughout each match, your Shield meter is displayed as a blue line. Here, it can be seen near the bottom-center of the screen, above the Health meter. However, the location of the

Health and Shield meters will vary, based on what gaming platform you're using.

Shield Potion

This is one of the loot powerups you can find, acquire, and consume during a match. Within a single slot of your backpack, you can hold multiple Shield Potions, and then consume them, one at a time, as you deem necessary. Like all loot items, Shield Potions can be found within chests, within Supply Drops, acquired from defeated enemies, or sometimes found lying on the ground (out in the open). You may also find them being sold from a Vending Machine.

Each time you drink a Shield Potion, your Shield meter increases by 50 (up to a maximum of 100). Drink two in a row to fully activate and replenish your soldier's shields. This item takes several seconds to consume, during which time your soldier is vulnerable to attack.

Shields

In addition to Health Points, one of the things that can help keep you alive during a match are shields. At the start of a match, you do not have shields and your Shield meter will be at zero. Shields will protect you against enemy attacks. However, shields will *not* protect you against falls. How much added protection you'll have will depend on the level of your Shield meter.

When you have active shields and you receive damage, first your Shield meter will get depleted, based on the severity of the damage. Then, if you receive additional damage once your Shield meter reaches zero, your Health meter will be negatively impacted.

The moment both your Health meter and Shield meter are empty, you'll be eliminated from the match. All of the weapons, ammo, loot, and resources you collected during the match will be lost.

Whenever you find and consume a Small Shield Potion, Shield Potion, Slurp Juice, or Chug Jug, your shields will be activated or replenished. As soon as you find a loot item that will activate or replenish your shields, use it. Consuming one Chug Jug, for example, will activate your shields or replenish your Shield meter to 100 percent.

As you enter into the End Game portion of a match, ideally you want your Health meter and Shield meter to be at 100 percent. Plus, have at least one or two loot items on hand that will replenish your health and shields when you take damage.

Shifty Shafts

Found at map coordinates D7, in addition to the buildings and structures you can see above ground, this region contains a maze-like collection of underground mining tunnels.

There are a few homes in the outskirts of Shifty Shafts to explore. Each contains items worth collecting.

You'll find chests, as well as weapons, ammo, and loot on the ground within the mine tunnels. If you see a crate to stand on, do so. Always remember that you have the advantage by being even slightly higher than your opponent when you engage in a firefight. Crouch down and tiptoe your way through the mine tunnels, so enemies won't hear you approaching. As you approach a turn or intersection, have your weapon drawn and be ready to encounter an enemy soldier who's also exploring this region.

When viewing the Backpack Inventory screen, details about the selected weapon/item you're holding are displayed. Here, details about the Tactical Shotgun are displayed.

Shotguns can be used in close-range or mid-range combat situations, or even at a distance. (From a distance, they're harder to aim accurately than a rifle with a scope, for example.) When using a shotgun, always try for a headshot to inflict the most damage.

Slide Down Hills

Shotguns

Especially as you travel between points of interest on the island, you'll encounter hills and mountains. Surrounding many tall hills and mountains are steep cliffs. If you attempt to leap off of a cliff, you will either take damage (lose HP), or get injured so badly you'll be eliminated from the match.

Perhaps the most useful type of weapon offered on the island is any type of shotgun. There are many types to choose from, and shotguns are more powerful than a pistol.

Instead of jumping off a cliff, walk to the extreme edge, and then slide down it by pointing your directional controller inward. Sliding down even the steepest hill or cliff is safe. Keep in mind, you can't slide off of ramps, stairs, roofs, or towers, however.

Slurp Juice

As you drink each Slurp Juice, your HP and shield strength increase by one point every second (for up to 25 seconds). While you're drinking, your soldier must be standing still and is vulnerable to attack.

Within a single slot of your backpack, you're able to carry around multiple Slurp Juices that you can then consume, one at a time, as you need them. Your Health and Shield meters both max out at 100 points. If your Health meter is at 85 and your Shields are at 80, consuming a

Slurp Juice will bring both meters back to 100, but not higher.

Small Shield Potion

A Small Shield Potion is less powerful than a Shield Potion. These are two separate types of items, and if you have one or more of each, they will require two slots within your backpack.

Consuming a Small Shield Potion increases your shield strength by 25 (up to a maximum of 100), but it takes several seconds to drink, during which time your soldier is vulnerable to attack.

SMGs (Sub Machine Guns)

This is another category of weapon available on the island. There are multiple variations of SMGs, which tend to offer a large MAG Capacity and can spew out many rounds of ammunition per second. The farther away you are from your target, the less accurate your aim will be.

SMGs are ideal for close-range to mid-range combat, but they work okay as long-range weapons too. They're particularly useful for shooting at and destroying ramps, structures, or walls.

Sniper Attack

Fortnite: Battle Royale includes several types of sniper rifles and rifles with scopes. These are superior for long-range attacks because you can aim them very precisely.

A sniper attack (using a rifle with a scope) works best when your soldier is safe behind some type of protective barrier and is both far away and higher up than the target. For improved accuracy, crouch down when aiming your weapon, use the scope for aiming, and pull the trigger when your target is centered within the crosshairs.

When you aim a rifle with a scope attached to it, you'll really be able to zoom in and target an opponent who is far away.

Sniper Rifles

A sniper rifle is a rifle with a scope, so it can be used to accurately target enemies from a distance. A direct hit, especially a headshot, will be devastating to your opponent.

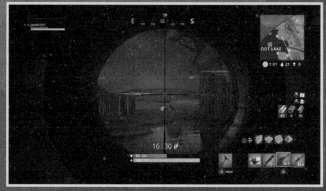

Take a moment to carefully aim your rifle when using a scope. A sniper rifle has a small MAG Capacity and slow Reload Time, so if your first one or two shots don't hit their target, take cover to avoid getting shot at while the weapon reloads.

As with all powerful weapons, they're only useful if you have compatible ammunition on hand. Collect appropriate ammunition throughout a match, even if you don't yet have a Sniper Rifle. This type of weapon will be extremely useful during the End Game portion of a match, but can be used anytime to knock off an opponent.

Snobby Shores

Don't forget to search the attics and basements (when applicable) of each mansion. This is typically where you'll discover chests.

Located at map coordinates A5, this is where the rich people who formerly populated the island once lived. The area contains several lovely waterfront mansions, each of which offers multiple floors and many rooms to explore.

Located near this region are two mountains. In Season 4, one mountain contained a secret base that's hidden inside the mountain, while the other contains a home. (This base may be removed from the game in Season 5 or later.)

Before entering any mansion or home, listen carefully for noises coming from the inside. Also, peek through the windows, and make sure the coast is clear. Don't forget, you can always surprise an enemy by shooting through a window. If you know someone is already inside, and you're not afraid to confront them, consider entering any mansion or home through the garage or back door, as opposed to the front door. Be unpredictable.

In addition to searching the mansions, be sure to search the security buildings and storage buildings location near many of the mansions.

Within the mountain, at map coordinates C5.5, you'll discover a hidden base. Build a ramp to the top of the mountain to reach its secret entrance.

Smash open this garage that's located on the mountain, and then travel down into the heart of the mountain.

Explore the entire area of this hidden base. You'll find several chests, along with plenty of other weapons, ammo, and loot.

There's also a giant missile here. The purpose of this base and the missile are a mystery that was revealed at the end of Season 4 (when the missile launched), and at the beginning of Season 5 (when the rift in the sky created by the missile was explained).

Solo Mode

Solo Mode in *Fortnite: Battle Royale* means you must act alone on the island as you attempt to outlive (and potentially defeat) up to 99 other opponents, without any assistance from a partner or squad of allies. Choose the Solo game play mode from the Lobby before a match.

Sound FX Volume

By listening carefully to the sound effects in the game, you can often determine the location of enemies and how close they are to you. Hearing all of the sound effects clearly will give you an advantage, so always pay attention to what you're hearing, as well as what you're seeing.

Sound effects play a crucial role in *Fortnite: Battle Royale*. For example, every soldier causes the sound of footsteps to be heard when they walk, run, or tiptoe. Smashing objects also makes noise, as do the sounds of explosions or weapon fire. Every time a door is opened or closed, everyone who is nearby will hear the squeak of the hinges.

Watching others, especially highly skilled and experienced gamers, play *Fortnite: Battle Royale* can be extremely useful for helping you develop your own game play strategies. Figure out what other players are doing right when it comes to fighting, building, and exploring, for example, and try to mimic or improve upon their strategies in the future. One of the final moments of an End Game is shown here. Two soldiers remain in the match. Each is firing at the other from their respective forts, using the most powerful, long-range weapons at their disposal.

From the Settings menu, choose the Audio submenu option, and then turn up the Sound FX Volume option to a level that allows you to hear everything. Consider using headphones or a gamer's headset when playing *Fortnite: Battle Royale* to ensure all of the sound effects are crystal clear.

Spectator Mode

Getting eliminated from a match can be a depressing and often frustrating experience. Instead of getting annoyed and immediately exiting back to the Lobby, stick around and stay in Spectator Mode, so you can watch the rest of the match.

Like any competent player, this one defeats her enemies, and then stocks up on ammo, more powerful weapons, and loot as the End Game quickly approaches.

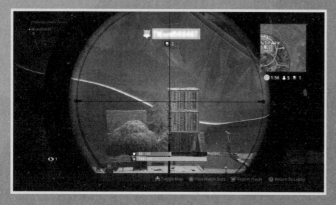

Especially during the End Game, knowing the location where your last few adversaries are hiding is essential. Use the scope of your long-range weapon to spy on each remaining enemy and plan your final attacks.

Spray Paint Tag Emote

To use a spray paint tag, you must unlock individual tag designs prior to a match, and then add one or more of them to your Emote menu from the Locker. Your soldier can access up to six emotes from the Emotes menu. This includes your choice of spray paint tags, dance moves, and/or graphic emotes.

This is one of three types of emotes that your soldier can use throughout a match. A spray paint tag allows you to quickly paint a selected design onto any flat surface in the game, such as a wall, tree, roof, or vehicle. During a match, access the Emote menu, stand in front of the object you want to paint, and then select your tag design.

From the Locker, select one Emote box. A menu of available emotes that you've already unlocked (and that are currently available to you) is displayed. Choose one that will go into the selected Emote slot.

If you have time, use the same or different tag designs multiple times at the same location to create original ways to leave your mark.

Squad Up

When playing the Squad game play mode, this is the process of inviting up to three of your friends to play with you on the same team.

If three friends aren't available, but you still want to play using the Squad Mode, select the Fill option, and the game will match you up with additional players. When playing with one or more allies, communication during the match is essential. Either use a gamer's headset so you can talk in real-time, or rely on using the Quick Chat menu.

Squads Mode

This is one of the permanent game play modes offered in *Fortnite: Battle Royale*. It allows you to team up with up to three friends or team members. You'll work together to defeat all of the enemy soldiers on the island, so you and/or one or more of your team members becomes the last person or people alive at the end of a match.

From the Lobby before a match begins, select the Game Play Modes menu. The option for it is displayed directly above the Play option. From the Choose Game Mode menu, select Squads. Then from the Lobby, invite your team members to join you or accept a friend's invitation.

By selecting the Fill option after selecting the Squads game play mode, the game itself will match you up with three other (random) players. Throughout the match, the username, Health meter, and Shield meter for each team member is displayed on the screen. Here, this information can be seen in the top-left corner of the game screen. This may vary, based on what gaming platform you're using.

Once a Squads mission begins, you can exchange weapons, ammo, and loot with your team members, and keep tabs on each other's location. You definitely want to work together during a match as much as possible.

You can identify your team members by their appearance. Their username also appears directly over their head. When you're not close to your team members, a message appears on the screen showing you what direction they're in. Plus, you can identify them on the location map that's displayed on the screen.

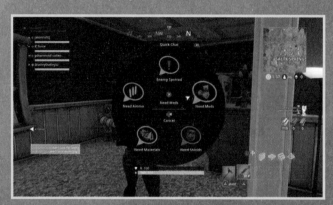

During a Duos or Squads match, if you and your teammates are not using gamer's headsets and can't speak to each other, use the Quick Chat menu to exchange messages.

Stink Bombs

When tossed, these bombs generate a cloud of yellow smoke that has an awful smell. It'll make your enemies fun for cover and receive damage at the same time. For every half-second an enemy is stuck in the stink cloud generated by the bomb, his health or shields drop by five points. The stink cloud lasts for nine seconds.

Stone (Also Known as Brick)

Stone is one of the three types of resources you're able to collect and build with during a match. Stone is stronger than wood, but slower to build with. It is, however, weaker than metal (and faster to build with than metal).

During a match, collect stone by smashing at stone piles with your pickaxe, smashing at brick walls with your pickaxe, collecting them from defeated enemies, or by finding and grabbing brick icons that are scattered around the island. Brick and stone are the same resource.

Storage Depot

This cargo storage facility (which is found at map coordinates H4.5, but not labeled on the map) contains many storage containers. The area somewhat resembles Junk Junction, in that there are piles of storage containers everywhere, which transforms the ground level into a maze-like area.

Inside the cargo containers, as well as above them, and within the neighboring buildings, you'll discover lots of useful items to collect, so you can expand your arsenal. The containers make great hiding spots, or you can booby-trap them using traps or remote explosives, for example, and then try to lure your enemies inside. Your best bet, however, is to stay high up, so you can look and shoot downwards at your enemies below.

Land on top of this building and then smash your way through the roof to open the chest that's below. If you're landing here from the Battle Bus, you can see the glow of this chest from the air.

Be sure to check the buildings located at each of the four corners of this area. Inside, you're apt to discover chests and other goodies.

On ground level, the position of the containers creates a maze-like area you'll need to navigate through. Inside the containers, you'll often find great stuff to grab.

To quickly reach higher ground, build a bridge and get yourself to the top of the containers.

The containers with two open ends can be used as a tunnel as you make your way through the maze on ground level. The containers with just one open door provide excellent shelter.

Once you're high up, shoot down at enemies who are still scampering around at ground level.

Storm

One of the challenges you'll encounter on the island is the deadly storm. As a match progresses, the storm expands and moves, taking up more and more of the island and making more of the land uninhabitable. This forces the surviving soldiers to keep moving in order to stay within the safe area.

As you look at the island map, the safe area is within the circle shown on the map. If two circles are seen, the outer circle represents the current safe area, and the inner circle shows you where the storm will be expanding to next. Thus, the area within the smaller circle will be the safe area once the storm moves again.

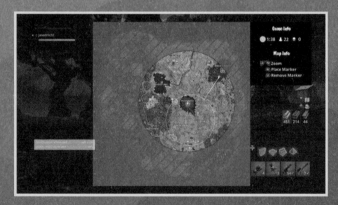

The area displayed on the map in pink has already been ravaged by the storm.

As long as you have HP, you can stay within the storm-ravaged areas for a short time.

However, doing so will cause your Shield meter, and then your Health meter, to take a hit. During later stages of a match, the damage inflicted by staying in the storm-ravaged (unsafe) areas increases, and damage happens faster. If you wind up staying within the storm for too long, you'll perish!

If you must enter into the storm, make sure your Health and Shield meters are maxed out in order to stay alive longer. The white triangle on the map shows your current location, and the white line shows the fastest and most direct route to follow in order to escape the storm.

One of the fastest ways to escape the storm if you get caught within it is to use a Launch Pad (or Jetpack).

Storm Progression

Starting within moments after landing on the island, the deadly storm will materialize and start to make more and more of the island's landmass uninhabitable. Every few minutes, the storm will expand and move. A timer will inform you when the storm will be expanding next. You can determine the storm's movement by frequently referring to the island map.

Storm Rider (Storm Trooper)

Entering into the storm for a short amount of time will cause your Shield or Health meter to take a hit, but the exposure won't be lethal if you exit the storm before your Health meter reaches zero. For this reason, some gamers choose to hide in the storm for short periods of time or go into the storm to reposition themselves and launch a surprise attack on an enemy. When you use the storm to your tactical advantage, you're referred to as a "Storm Rider" or "Storm Trooper."

Structures

There are many types of structures on the island. As you encounter each type, figure out how you can best utilize it to your advantage. Do you need a place to hide? Are you looking for a location that offers a tactical advantage from which to launch an attack? Do you need to locate weapons, ammo, or loot to increase your arsenal?

Pre-created structures (some containing chests, weapons, ammo, loot, and resource icons) can be found throughout the island, plus you can build your own structures anywhere—not just within the various points of interest.

As you explore the island, especially within the various points of interest, you'll discover many types of pre-built structures including bridges, buildings, cabins, churches, clock towers, crypts, factories, farmhouses, homes, lodges, mansions, mines, offices, prisons, restaurants, silos, stables, stores, and watch towers.

Using any type of explosive weapons, such as grenades, remote explosives (shown), or a projectile explosive weapon (a rocket launcher or grenade launcher), for example, any pre-built structure can be destroyed. Whenever you fully destroy a structure, anyone inside will receive damage or could wind up defeated as a result of their injuries. This is what a cabin looked like before remote explosives were placed and set off.

After placing three remote explosives and detonating them, this is what remains of the cabin.

Within any pre-built structure, anything inside, such as furniture, appliances, or items, can be smashed and destroyed. If you smash something made from wood, such as a wall or staircase, your wood collection will increase. If you smash something made from brick, such as a wall or fireplace, your stone collection will increase. If you smash something made of metal, such as a fence or kitchen appliance, your metal collection will increase.

Keep in mind, you are able to build walls, ramps, stairs, or even mini-forts within, on top of, or adjacent to pre-created structures. For example, you can build a ramp or stairs to reach an otherwise inaccessible area, or build extra walls around yourself to remain extra safe while hiding inside a pre-created structure.

Supply Drop

Always be on the lookout for Supply Drops. They typically land just outside of points of interest on the map. When you discover one landing nearby, approach with caution, and only if you need to expand your arsenal with some potentially powerful and rare weapons.

Instead of approaching a Supply Drop, many experienced players find a good hiding spot near the landing site and wait to ambush enemy soldiers who attempt to reach the Supply Drop. Any long-range weapon, particularly a sniper rifle (or rifle with a scope) or a grenade launcher, can be used to launch a surprise attack from a distance.

Tilted Towers

Found at map coordinates D5.5, the first thing you'll notice when you enter Tilted Towers is that it's one of the most popular places on the island, so you're sure to encounter many enemy soldiers here. Be prepared to fight your way through each of the buildings and to continue the firefights on the streets.

If you're planning to land in this area from the Battle Bus, be the first person to wind up on the roof of the clock tower, and then smash your way down toward ground level. Along the way, you'll discover at least three chests by the time you reach ground level.

To easily defeat a few enemies here in Tilted Towers, find a safe position near the top of a building, and then use a shotgun, sniper rifle, or a rifle with a scope to shoot at enemies below. Notice there's an unopened chest within the window in the building across from this soldier. Simply aim your weapon at the chest and wait for an unsuspecting enemy to approach and open it. As soon as you see the enemy in your sights, start shooting.

Stick to the higher ground here in Tilted Towers as much as you can.

Each building contains multiple floors and at least several rooms. Don't be surprised if you find enemies hiding. Be extra cautious if you enter a room after hearing footsteps or the sound of a door opening or closing.

Because Tilted Towers is such a popular landing spot, you probably won't be the only person landing on a building's roof, if that's where you decide to go. Since you're unarmed when you land, either be the first person to grab a weapon that's lying on the ground or be prepared to do battle using your pickaxe. If you see the roofs of the buildings are crowded, land slightly outside of Tilted Towers, build up your arsenal, and then enter this dangerous area.

If you're brave enough to wander around outside at ground level within Tilted Towers, you'll be rewarded if you're the first to stumble upon the chests, weapons, loot, and other items lying out in the open. However, watch out for snipers from above, as well as other enemies who are also on ground level, hiding, and waiting to ambush any soldier attempting to approach an item, such as this chest.

When you enter into a crowded building and begin exploring, make sure you don't get trapped in a corner (or confined space) with no way to escape. There are a lot of small rooms where you could get yourself trapped, especially if you haven't yet collected the right weapons to engage in firefights. Expect Tilted Towers to get a face lift at the start of Season 5.

Tiptoe

When you have your soldier crouch down and move in any direction, this allows him to tiptoe. This is much slower than walking or running, but it makes a lot less noise, especially when indoors. Crouching down also improves your aim when firing any type of weapon.

Tires

Tires can't be collected or smashed for resources, but a soldier can jump on them to gain extra height and use them like a trampoline in order to reach a higher area.

Tomato Town

Aside from a pizza restaurant, taco stand, and gas station, this area contains several homes to explore. You'll find Tomato Town at map coordinates G4. The interesting part of this point of interest are the tunnels and bridges that lead into and out of this region.

Check out both levels of the pizza restaurant. An assortment of random weapons, ammo, and loot can be found here.

Anytime you see a home with a cellar door on the outside, smash open the door and explore each room of the basement. You will almost always find a chest.

The gas station within Tomato Town doesn't typically contain too much of anything that's useful on the inside. However, check the roof and what surrounds this structure. Don't try hiding within any of the single floor gas stations on the island, including this one. An enemy will easily see you inside and can shoot at you through one of the many windows.

Around the shoreline of the island, you'll discover a bunch of tall watch towers. Each is a different shape. What they all have in common is that they're large. The tower shown here is located near map coordinates B1. As you can see, it looks like a giant crab.

This tunnel which leads in and out of Tomato Town is one of the more unusual things to see in the area. Inside the tunnel, you'll discover loot. About halfway through the tunnel is a stairway that leads upward. Inside the stairway you will find more loot. On the opposite end of Tomato Town, a bridge offers another route for getting into or out of this area. Be sure to check on the bridge, as well as below it, for useful items.

When you encounter one of these towers (this one is on the shoreline, just outside of Wailing Woods near map coordinates J3), either land on the roof after departing from the Battle Bus or build a ramp to reach the top of it and then smash your way downwards. See what you discover inside. If you're approaching from ground level, you may discover a door to get inside. Smashing the tower with a pickaxe allows you to gather resources.

Towers

Traps

Once you pick up one or more traps, instead of taking up a regular slot within your backpack, an icon for it will appear as part of the Building

Mode menu. To later set the trap, enter into Building Mode and select the trap.

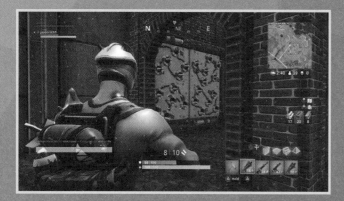

A trap can be set up on a structure's floor, wall, or ceiling. Traps can also be placed on ramps. Based on where it's placed, it will become a "spike trap," "wall trap," or "ceiling zapper" trap. When an opponent accidentally activates the hidden trap, they'll receive mega-damage. Just make sure you don't set off the trap yourself once you've activated it, or you'll be the one getting hurt!

Trees

Trees are the greatest source of wood on the island. You'll discover them in smaller quantities within many points of interest. Groups of trees, and even small forests, can be found in the outskirts of many points of interest.

The largest trees can be found in and around Wailing Woods (near map coordinates I3). Your soldier can hide behind or at the top of most

trees or use their pickaxe to chop 'em down to collect wood. When chopping a tree (or any resource for that matter), aim the pickaxe at the target that appears to generate the most units of that resource.

Turbo Building

After turning on this feature from the Settings menu, once you enter into Building Mode and choose a building piece and resource type, as long as you hold down the build trigger button on the controller (or keyboard/mouse), that building piece will keep getting built and placed until you release the build button or resources run out. Using this feature makes building a ramp or placing walls around you a much faster and easier process.

Twitch Prime Packs

Epic Games has teamed up with Twitch.tv and Amazon.com to periodically offer free, downloadable item packs. To redeem them, you must set up a free Twitch.tv account, and also be a paid Amazon Prime member.

A typical Twitch Prime Pack includes an outfit, matching pickaxe and glider design, and emotes, along with other items for customizing your soldier. For more information, visit www.twitch.tv/prime/fortnite.

Unlabeled Points of Interest

In addition to the more than 20 points of interest that are labeled on the map, there are a growing number of locations that are not labeled, but that contain interesting structures or buildings to explore, items to collect, or ways of gathering extra weapons, ammo, loot, and/or resources.

You'll often find unlabeled points of interest along the outer edges (coastline) of the island and when traveling between labeled points of interest. The following are just a few of the unlabeled areas you might want to visit during your next match.

Located at map coordinates C5, you'll discover two indoor sports arenas, along with a few other structures that are not labeled on the map.

The motel (located between map coordinates D2 and E2) is popular because within the former guestrooms, as well as in and around the other structures, you're apt to find a lot of really good weapons, ammo, and loot, especially if you're the first one to explore this area. It's not too far away from Anarchy Acres.

Around map coordinates E9 is where you'll find a cluster of buildings, one of which is a dance club.

This is all that remains of an old mansion found near map coordinates C2 (outside of Junk Junction). You'll definitely discover chests, as well as other loot among the ruins.

Here at map coordinates I5, there's an RV park that's surrounded by a few structures. You're more apt to find useful items within the structures, but if you navigate your way around the RVs and picnic tables, you'll find weapons, ammo, and loot lying on the ground and on the roofs of some RVs.

If you check out the area near map coordinates D8, this small area contains a few houses and a taco restaurant. From a distance, you'll notice the wooden tower that's shaped like a chair. Here, the soldier is standing on it.

There's a container storage depot found near map coordinates H4.5. This one has a bridge overhead that you can walk along in order to get and stay higher than your enemies.

Inside what looks like a warehouse is this bizarre movie set. It's located near map coordinates C1.5. On the upper level there's a chest. Take a detour from Junk Junction and see for yourself what's here.

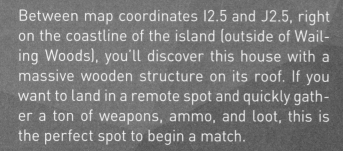

Between map coordinates I2.5 and J2.5, right on the coastline of the island (outside of Wailing Woods), you'll discover this house with a massive wooden structure on its roof. If you want to land in a remote spot and quickly gather a ton of weapons, ammo, and loot, this is the perfect spot to begin a match.

Land on top of this structure and smash your way down as you explore. Then make your way inland, avoiding other points of interest during the early stages of a match. You'll be able to stockpile plenty of resources and ammo, while avoiding enemies.

During Season 4, in conjunction with The World Cup Soccer tournament, a massive sports arena with a soccer field was added near map coordinates C2. When you visit here, there are many areas within and around the arena to explore, plus lots of great stuff to collect.

V-Bucks

This is virtual currency within the game. It can be exchanged for items from the Item Shop, or to purchase a Battle Pass, or unlock a Battle Pass Tier. There are two ways to acquire V-Bucks. You can achieve goals within the game to earn 100 V-Bucks at a time, or you can purchase them (using real money) from the Shop.

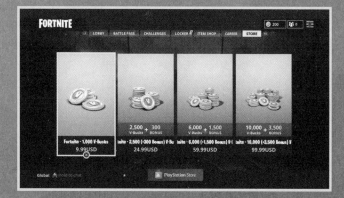

V-Bucks are sold in bundles of 1,000 ($9.99), 2,800 ($24.99), 7,500 ($59.99), or 13,500 ($99.99).

Vending Machine

Located throughout the island—not just within points of interest—are Vending Machines. Using wood, stone, or metal resources you've collected (not V-Bucks), purchase rare and powerful weapons and loot that are sold from these machines. While the location of the machines is typically consistent from match to match, what's sold within them is not.

Displayed on the front of each Vending Machine are scrolling graphics that show the selection of items available from that machine, as well as each item's price (in resources, not V-Bucks). This Vending Machine can be found in Greasy Grove.

Once you know what items are sold from a particular Vending Machine, if you don't have enough resources on hand to buy the item(s) you want, go collect the necessary resources and return to that Vending Machine. You'll discover this Vending Machine outside of a small structure within Loot Lake.

To make a purchase, walk directly in front of the Vending Machine and when the item you want is displayed, press the Buy button on your controller (or keyboard/mouse). The item will be added to your Backpack Inventory.

However, if your backpack is already full, you will need to drop an item before acquiring a new one. Lucky Landing is where you'll stumble upon this Vending Machine.

Anytime you're standing out in the open, in front of a Vending Machine, watch out for enemy attacks. Consider building walls around you and the Vending Machine for protection, especially if you know multiple enemy soldiers are in the area. If you're not careful, as soon as you make a purchase, an enemy will attack you, eliminate you from the match, and collect your latest purchases (along with everything else you collected during that match).

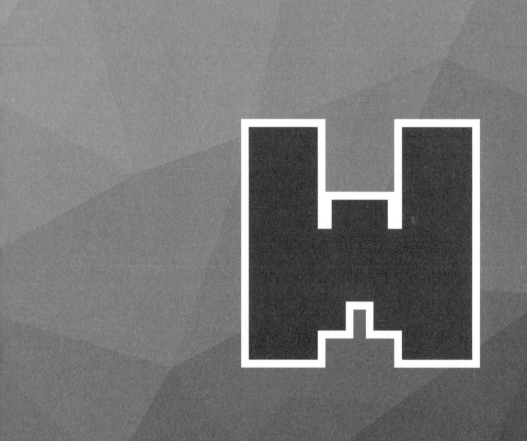

Wailing Woods

As you're wandering through the forest within Wailing Woods, which is found at map coordinates I3, be sure to collect plenty of wood using your pickaxe. In the center of this area is a hedge maze. Make your way through the maze to discover wooden structures that contain items worth collecting.

Near the center of Wailing Woods, you'll stumble upon the entrance to the hedge maze.

Follow the hedge maze in search of the tower. Along the way, be on the lookout for chests, weapons, and of course enemy soldiers who may be hiding around any turn.

Search the tower to find chests and other loot.

Climb on top of the hedges so you're higher up than soldiers walking through the maze. This makes it easier to acquire clear shots.

Take a short detour to the outskirts of Wailing Woods, and you'll discover this massive wooden tower near the coastline. Find the secret door, go inside, climb upwards, and collect the loot that's inside!

During Season 4, one of the mysteries on the island was found within Wailing Woods. Located on the ground, it looks like an underground bunker entrance, but it could not be opened, smashed, blasted, or damaged. Perhaps the answer to where this entrance leads or what's inside will be revealed in Season 5 or beyond.

Walk

Walking is one of the ways a soldier moves around the island. Running is faster, while tiptoeing is slower, but makes less noise.

Weapon Rarity

Every weapon available in *Fortnite: Battle Royale* has the ability to inflict damage and defeat your adversaries. Some can also easily destroy structures. Each weapon is rated based on several criteria, including its rarity. Weapons are color-coded with a hue around them to showcase their rarity.

Weapons with a gray hue are "Common."

Weapon with a green hue are "Uncommon."

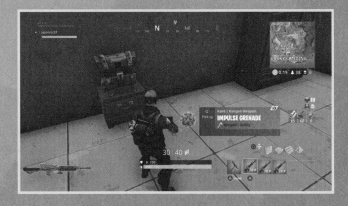

Weapons with a blue hue are "Rare."

Weapons with a purple hue are "Epic."

"Legendary" weapons (with an orange hue) are hard to find, extra powerful, and very rare. If you're able to obtain one, grab it!

It is possible to collect several of the same weapon, but each could have a different rarity.

If you collect two of the same weapon, and one is rare, but the second is legendary, definitely keep the legendary weapon and trade the other for something else when you find a replacement.

Weapons

There are many types of weapons that you'll discover and can grab on the island. Before engaging in a firefight, however, consider:

- The types of weapons currently in your backpack and available to you.
- The amount of ammo you currently have for each weapon. (Be sure to pick up as much ammo as you can throughout each match.)
- Your distance from an adversary.
- Your surroundings, and whether or not your weapon will need to destroy a barrier, fortress wall, or shielding before it can inflict damage on an enemy.
- Your own skill level as a gamer, and your speed when it comes to selecting, targeting/aiming, and then firing your weapon.

In each weapon category, up to a dozen or more different types of weapons may become accessible to you. Epic Games regularly tweaks the selection of weapons available, as well as the capabilities of each weapon.

Wood

Wood is one of the three resources you'll need to collect during a match. When it comes to building, wood is the fastest resource to work with. It's great for quickly constructing ramps, or for creating small forts that'll offer basic protection if attacked. Both stone and metal are stronger materials that better resist incoming attacks, but they're slower to build with.

Three of the easiest ways to collect wood include:

1. Look for wood icons to collect and grab bundles of wood. They're found out in the open, as well as within chests.
2. Use your pickaxe to smash any wooden object, including trees, and the walls or roofs of homes or structures.
3. Anytime you defeat an enemy, collect all the resources that soldier has left behind.

Wood pallets that are scattered throughout the island (and found within many points of interest) provide a great source of wood. Smash wood pallets with your pickaxe.

FINAL THOUGHTS

Each time you participate in a *Fortnite: Battle Royale* match, your experience will be totally different for a variety of reasons. First and foremost, during each match, you'll come face-to-face with the soldiers being controlled by up to 99 other gamers.

Every gamer has his or her own strategies, skills, and experience when it comes to playing *Fortnite: Battle Royale*, so it's impossible to predict what actions and reactions you can expect from each player.

In addition, Epic Games continues to update *Fortnite: Battle Royale* with sometimes dramatic alterations to the island map; by introducing challenging new game play modes; by revealing exciting new storylines and subplots; by adding powerful new weapons and innovative types of new loot; and by making available eye-catching ways to showcase your soldier's appearance (with outfits, back bling, pickaxes, gliders, emotes, and other customizable elements).

In other words, this game continues to evolve. As a result, it never becomes boring, predictable, or easy to master. There's always something new to experience or discover. Plus, even if you get really good playing in Solo Mode, when you gather one or more friends to compete with you in the Duos or Squads game play modes (accessible from the Lobby), for example, the challenges and unpredictability within the game increase dramatically. Teamwork (including constant communication with your allies) becomes important.

Be sure to experience the other "limited time" game play modes that Epic Games introduces. Each offers a new twist to playing *Fortnite: Battle Royale* that's designed to test your skills.

Now that you've discovered tons of useful strategies to follow, what will make you a truly awesome gamer is a lot of practice!

Good luck, and more importantly, have fun!